6 50

INTRODUCTION TO
DEVELOPMENTAL PSYCHIATRY

INTRODUCTION
TO
DEVELOPMENTAL PSYCHIATRY

By

BEULAH C. BOSSELMAN, M.D.

Professor of Psychiatry
University of Illinois College of Medicine
Chicago, Illinois

IRA M. ROSENTHAL, M.D.

Professor of Pediatrics
University of Illinois College of Medicine
Chicago, Illinois

and

MARVIN SCHWARZ, M.D.

Child Psychiatrist and former Chief
Child Psychiatry Section
Presbyterian—St. Luke's Hospital
Chicago, Illinois

CHARLES C THOMAS • PUBLISHER
Springfield • Illinois • U.S.A.

Published and Distributed Throughout the World by

CHARLES C THOMAS • PUBLISHER

BANNERSTONE HOUSE

301-327 East Lawrence Avenue, Springfield, Illinois, U.S.A.

NATCHEZ PLANTATION HOUSE

735 North Atlantic Boulevard, Fort Lauderdale, Florida, U.S.A.

*With THOMAS BOOKS careful attention is given to all details of
manufacturing and design. It is the Publisher's desire to present books
that are satisfactory as to their physical qualities and artistic possibilities
and appropriate for their particular use. THOMAS BOOKS will be true
to those laws of quality that assure a good name and good will.*

Printed in the United States of America

0-5

Contents

v

INTRODUCTION TO
DEVELOPMENTAL PSYCHIATRY

Chapter I

Introduction

A STUDY of the processes and problems involved in human maturation furnishes observation of and insight into the origins of psychopathology. Such a study is appropriately presented early in the medical curriculum. This book has therefore been planned as a textbook for courses in introductory psychiatry. An attempt has been made to stress common developmental disturbances, to present psychiatric theory as a background for understanding the genesis and meanings of these maladjusted states, and to indicate their relationship to the pathology of neurotic and psychotic syndromes.

"Health" is the goal of all good medical practice. But health means more than mere freedom from disease. It implies the capacity to live to full potentiality, to participate, to enjoy, to give. This broader concept of health is particularly evident in pediatric and psychiatric practice.

The attainment of a capacity for a free, rich life depends upon the development of a feeling of significance in the world. Everyone needs to be "someone." Very early the baby tries to assert himself, to form satisfying relationships, to formulate a concept of what he is and what is expected of him. If he is handicapped in his first struggle for self-identification, he may become a so-called problem child, fighting and resisting the authorities which seem to threaten him. He may withdraw in a sense of hopeless alienation, consoling himself in his fantasies. In contrast, out of fear, the child may try so desperately to conform that he develops a rigid, compulsive personality, lacking the freedom of spontaneous behavior.

In psychiatry, as in other areas of medicine, the employment of measures to prevent the development of illness has the potential of providing improved levels of health with less expenditure

3

of effort and greater potential for success than can be obtained by elaborate subsequent therapeutic measures.

The newborn infant is a virtually helpless creature, largely oblivious and blind to his environment, unaware of his own person, and responsive only to such primitive experiences as hunger and pain. In contrast, the two-year-old child possesses well developed motor skills of locomotion and manipulation, has strong likes and dislikes and specific behavior regarding feeding, is frequently already toilet trained, and has usually mastered some of the basic essentials of his native language. The two-year-old, in addition, is keenly aware of himself as an individual, and has developed identification as a boy or girl. He distinguishes between various family members and strangers with appropriate behavior and emotional responses. He has already become aware of social attitudes and has developed the beginnings of "conscience." These achievements of the child during his first two years are dependent on the orderly maturation of the organism.

It is a well accepted fact that much of the maladjustment found in adult life is the result of early difficulty in growth and social adaptation. Inefficient and relatively unrealistic reactions become habitual and, once established, often continue as life-long handicaps. In the process of growing up it is important that the adaptive problems of each developmental phase be adequately mastered during that phase. If not, the child remains still absorbed in old struggles when his energy should be free for current adaptive tasks. The persistence of infantile patterns concerning authority and aggression and dependence into adolescence and adult life favors the development of psychiatric symptoms.

It is ordinarily during pre-adolescence and adolescence that the individual intensifies his infantile patterns of reaction while he is in the process of attempting resolution of his conflicts. By transposing the infantile structure into its adult derivatives the fortunate individual gradually emerges as a well adjusted, mature adult.

Skillful reconstruction of personality development is a difficult task. It demands of the physician familiarity with the normal patterns of maturation in our culture. It is essential for the physician to understand the somatic and psychic responses by which the child at first copes with the frustrations of his essential physical needs, makes adjustments to parental and other figures in the family setting, and develops a consistent concept of himself.

It is in the young child that the physician can observe frank reactions undisguised by the protective shields developed later. Disorders of feeding, of elimination, of sleep, of social behavior; retardations in learning; phobic and obsessive attitudes, are common symptoms in childhood. Often such symptoms are relatively mild and transient. They may represent a more or less realistic protest of the young person against the deprivations and restraints imposed by his caretakers, and thus indicate the presence of a situation of crisis with which the child is attempting to deal, using the resources at his disposal. It is in the process of dealing with such crises that the child should undergo normal maturation. If a child has adequate resources to face and resolve a conflictual experience, these crises then become the basis for optimal development. In contrast, the child lacking such resources at this state of growth may develop self-perpetuating psychopathologic adaptive mechanisms.

These syndromes of maladjustment, apart from their importance as possible forerunners of adult psychiatric disturbance, are an object of immediate concern to the pediatrician. Behavior disorders constitute a major focus of the "new" pediatrics. It is one of the challenges of medical practice that the physician by direct and indirect techniques may contribute significantly to the emotional health and stability of his patients. This is particularly true in the field of pediatrics. On the other hand, the physician may actually contribute to pathological responses by his encouragement of unsound and naive child rearing practices. He may, furthermore, by his failure to recognize the significance of the behavior of the child and the disturbed relationships within the family, lose an opportunity to influence favorably the individual's development.

Developmental difficulties of early life result from interacting biologic and environmental factors. The process of growing up does in itself impose frustrations and demands. Once out of the womb, the infant is subjected to more or less discomfort and to delay in the satisfaction of his needs. The impositions of the outer world increase progressively and he is expected more and more to recognize and behave acceptably in complex interpersonal relationships. As his perception sharpens and his interest becomes focused externally he learns to manipulate and to communicate in ways that allow satisfaction of his needs and at the same time give him a sense of participation and involvement with the people about him, particularly his mother.

Some infants seem by nature better fitted for these adaptive interactions than do others. Such qualities as intelligence, physical strength and reserve and capacity for homeostatic adjustment are of importance. Individual reaction-patterns reveal themselves early in the infant's behavior, and such behavior in turn influences the reactions of the parents. An irritable, overactive baby tends to bring out tension and anxiety in his mother, whereas sluggishness and unresponsiveness may favor disappointment and possibly neglect. These parental attitudes then become part of the child's environment and further influence his own concept of himself as he develops awareness of what people expect of him and how they feel about him. Such circular interpersonal mechanisms are commonly encountered throughout later life as well as during early development. An individual's behavior, through its effect upon others, may produce its own dampening or intensification. It is therefore often difficult to distinguish between primary and secondary effects.

Parental attitudes are, of course, determined not only by the infant's innate characteristics but to a large extent by the parents' own emotional state and by the total family situation. For this reason, different children in one family may be exposed to quite different environments. For example, a first child may arrive unplanned at a time of financial stress and strain which no longer exist when later children are born. The last of several children, or the only boy in a family of girls, may be overly pampered. Competition among siblings varies greatly, as does the tendency of the parents, on the basis of their own needs, to identify themselves with one or another of their children. Cognizance of these subtle situational differences makes it unwise to attribute developmental disorders of children to simple inborn qualities.

The impact of the environment is greatly influenced by cultural tradition. Children reared in a rigid patriarchal system receive a different early impression of social and family relationships than do those reared by parents steeped in "liberal" permissive attitudes of present-day American culture. Family and group attitudes toward obedience and conformity, the values which they place on activity versus passivity, and their interpretations of masculinity and femininity, are a few of the variables to which the child responds. Acting directly on him and indirectly through the family, such variable factors affect the nature of the child's—and later the adult's—psychological problems.

We shall therefore attempt, in this presentation of developmental crises, to evaluate the interacting effects of individual endowment, family milieu and cultural background. The adaptive responses of the child and adolescent in these crises will be examined as determinants of the adult life pattern. In this way the book will, we hope, serve as preparation for subsequent courses in clinical psychiatry. It is evident that no attempt has been made to be complete or encyclopedic. The material in the presentation should be supplemented by lectures, case presentations, discussion periods and additional reading.

Chapter II

The Feeding Experience

THE PRIMARY focus of the feeding of infants and young children is the provision of nutrients optimal for energy requirements and growth. It is also evident, however, that the feeding relationship is necessarily closely related to the personality development of the child. The feeding experience not only provides satisfaction of bodily needs for nourishment but it also is a source of security and pleasure. The child who is not being adequately nourished or who, in the process, is not securing adequate emotional gratification has a feeding problem. In the ordinary course of events, feeding experiences lend themselves to the establishment of a warm, comforting relationship of the child to his mother.

This relationship develops slowly and passes through many phases. In the neonatal period the infant is completely dependent upon the mother and must adapt to her mode of feeding him. As he becomes older and learns to differentiate himself from his environment he develops a more active role in the feeding relationship. He exerts more discrimination in his demands for food and in the manner in which the food is presented. In the process, the child begins to reject particular foods and to resist feeding under strange circumstances. This is particularly evident in relation to spoon feeding, but it also manifests itself in his activity in regard to the breast or bottle. He begins to show a more active, possessive or, at times, rejective behavior. There is a gradual shift from automatic reflex patterns of feeding to consciously self-determined eating patterns.[1] These changes reflect the neuromuscular development of the child and, at the same time, are associated with his evolution from a relatively passive, undifferentiated individual to a self-aware person. Meanwhile, the infant's mother must respond and adapt to this continually shifting feeding relationship.

[1] Spitz, Rene: *Yes and No*. International Universities Press, 1957 .

8

At the same time that the child tends to progress toward independence and control, he also has a tendency to vacillate between such progress and clinging to old and comfortable ways of functioning. This is first shown in his feeding behavior but also is evident, as we shall see later, in relation to all problems of maturation.

Disorders related to feeding are common in pediatric practice. The physician distinguishes feeding problems organic in origin from those based on a disturbed infantile relationship. It must be recognized that many serious disturbances of personality development may have their origin, at least in part, in faulty feeding practices.

Such symptoms as vomiting, anorexia, excessive appetite, abdominal pain, may originate from congenital or acquired disease of the gastro-intestinal tract. It is obvious that malformations of the gastro-intestinal tract can cause such disturbances. It should also be noted, however, that heart disease, pulmonary disease, renal insufficiency, severe infection, allergies, endocrine disturbances, and central nervous system conditions may cause complaints which center around feeding. Such complaints, though organic in origin, may be aggravated by secondary psychologic problems. The presence of a somatic handicap to good nutrition must be handled by the pediatrician with an awareness of the total problem.

> For example, J. N., aged nine months was found to be allergic to cow's milk, wheat, and a number of the other foods which he had been receiving. The pediatrician thereupon took him off all his former foods, substituting soybean product and adding a number of foods, which the child refused to eat. The baby's behavior became disturbed. He lost weight and regressed in socialization. The entire family became upset to such an extent that the mother sought psychiatric help. It was necessary for the pediatrician to modify the food restrictions with more regard to the child's attitudes.

It is equally important to recognize that, even in the absence of organic disease, serious as well as mild feeding disturbances occur in the infant. The physician encounters such complaints as vomiting, anorexia, refusal of specific foods, excessive milk drinking, and rumination in children free from somatic damage. The origin of these functional disturbances may not be immediately apparent. As the physician attempts to understand the nature of these symptoms, he looks at them as manifestations of reaction patterns, as responses of the young individual to his own biologic impulses in interaction with his environment.

From the earliest weeks of life, infants show individual qualities of behavior. This is often observed in their original approach to nursing. Some babies are hungrier than others. Some seem indifferent, preferring to sleep rather than to nurse. Some are tense and resistive; others are overly demanding. Mothers will sometimes interpret these responses as though they indicated a conscious process of resistance, and will react emotionally. Interactions may result, between mother and child, which do not favor good feeding habits.

Certain constitutional factors, either inherited or very early developed, predispose to nursing difficulties. The premature infant, or the child with a functional organic disturbance requires a great deal of patient care in the process of feeding.

Apart from recognizable constitutional or early acquired organic handicaps to adequate nursing, there is a less clearly defined quality which affects the infant's efficiency and apparent enjoyment in feeding. This quality might be characterized as his adaptive capacity. Some children, from the beginning, are more adequate in adaptive capacities than others. The change from uterine to extrauterine life imposes demands for adjustment to a greatly different situation. Nourishment is no longer automatically provided as needed, and the baby must fit himself into a schedule which imposes more or less delay and consequent frustration. Infants appear to differ constitutionally in the way they are equipped to meet this frustration. Those who are placid and comfortable are easily trained to a schedule. Others indicate a good deal of restlessness and discomfort in relation to any manipulation or deprivation. Because of this difference in temperament, all babies cannot be handled alike, and no categorical rules for infant feeding will apply in all cases This, perhaps, explains the changes from one generation to another in the advice offered to mothers in America regarding the feeding of infants. Rigid scheduling and demand feeding each develops proponents because each succeeds with a particular type of infant and family.

Children differ in their approach to feeding on the basis of physiologic fluctuation. The child's appetite varies with his growth period and the state of his health. The mother who is not aware of these to-be-expected variations may become worried when the appetite lags. At such times, she may coax or force the child to eat, and thus condition him to an unpleasant rather than a pleasant feeling about food.

Physical aspects of the nursing experience influence the degree of satisfaction of both mother and child. Breast feeding, when successful, provides optimal nutrition for the infant and an ideal basis for normal emotional development. Feeding her infant from the breast may be a satisfying and memorable experience for a mother. It provides a natural setting for physical contact of the infant with his mother, with oral gratification associated with sucking and feeding replacing the discomfort associated with hunger. Successful breast feeding requires that the infant play an active role in feeding.

Breast feeding, however, is not always successful. The percentage of infants fed successfully by breast tends to fall off in organized, industrial, prosperous communities. The reasons for the decline are not all apparent. Changing cultural patterns leading to rejection of breast feeding by mothers has played a major role. This accounts for the fact that many mothers never attempt breast feeding. Other factors account for its failure by mothers who do attempt it. Some of the failures are secondary to physical difficulties, such as breast abscesses, insufficient milk formation, or feebleness of the infant, as in prematurity. Emotional disturbance in the mother may prevent or interfere with the normal secretion of milk. Frustration with breast feeding sometimes results in the development of grave anxiety in the mother, interfering with her relationship with her infant. Many mothers who have been unsuccessful at breast feeding can successfully manage artificial feeding.

A family milieu is ideally suited for favoring individual development. Here the infant finds warmth and close protection combined with individuation and expectation of response to others. There is consistency and familiarity in his surroundings, with sufficient movement and variety in the relationships to stimulate and challenge him. His self-awareness and his awareness of others grow simultaneously. The exclusive preoccupation with satisfaction of his own needs for food and comfort become associated with interest in his mother and in others close to him. He learns to trust and to respond with affection.

Children reared in institutions, deprived of this favorable milieu, are seriously handicapped. Lacking warmth and personal stimulus they may remain self-absorbed, anxious, irritable, distrustful, and may develop irreversible personality defects.[1] Also, such children are subject to a high proportion of nutritional difficulties, even though the quality of the food given them is of the best.

Developmental difficulties, including feeding problems, occur, however, not only in institutional babies. Obviously, although a family constellation should contain the components favoring satisfactory infant adaptation, it is often lacking in many ways. The nature of the mother-child relationship is particularly important and this is sensitively reflected in the feeding behavior of the child. The over-anxious, tense mother often attaches her own anxieties to the adequate nourishment of her children, over-emphasizing correct intake to such a degree as to make it a painful procedure. Being unsure, she tends to act according to rules. She cannot trust herself to interpret adequately the infant's signals of satisfaction or distress. She feels comfortable only if he takes the exact amount prescribed, at the correct time intervals. Such mothers feel doubt as to their ability to care adequately for their children, and their concentration of concern on feeding presents a kind of over-compensation. Feeding becomes a duty that must be impersonally performed, rather than carried out in happy interaction with the child.

The young infant's horizons are narrow, and he cannot evaluate the meaning of his experiences. If he lacks individual attention and affection, he reacts as though to abandonment or

[1] Spitz, Rene: Hospitalism. *Psychoanalytic Study of the Child*, Vol. 2, p. 312, 1946.

rejection, whatever the cause of his deprived situation might be. This may be a situation or an attitude over which the parents have no control. For example, a mother who is ill and must be away from her child or is unavoidably preoccupied with other problems may have the warmest concern for her baby. The child may, nevertheless, show all the reactions of a rejected child. He may in such a situation express his disturbance by developing one or another kind of feeding disorder. This is often observed in hospitalized children, particularly if they are removed from the home during the age period of approximately eight to twenty-four months. During this period the baby is becoming aware of his mother as a familiar and consistent presence. In his attachment to his mother the infant develops an interest and a trust in another person. She is his point of contact to the world outside himself. When he suddenly loses this familiar contact, he reacts with disturbance, and this disturbance often interferes with his food intake and thus may complicate the illness for which he is hospitalized. Illustrations of this are common on any pediatrics ward. A child of vulnerable age, grieved and angry over separation from his mother, often refuses food or eats poorly during his adjustment period. The same reactions may occur at home if the mother leaves.

Every woman does not automatically accept the role of motherhood nor does she necessarily enjoy its social and biological aspects. Rejection of motherhood may result from obvious and practical disadvantages resulting from pain and physical discomfort, illegitimacy, large numbers of children, financial and health problems. Probably, however, of much greater importance are those subtle and ambivalent attitudes about motherhood which many women consciously or unconsciously harbor. Pregnancy may be accepted as a duty or responsibility, or used as a proof of femininity. The immature woman who still longs to be dependent may regard her infant with mixed feelings of affection and resentment. Insofar as the baby is her possession and she can be proud of him, she feels pleasure in him, but she finds it difficult to accept the restrictions which having a child imposes on her. The baby may be viewed as a competitor for her husband's love and also for the love of her own parents.

He may be considered as an interference with a way of life determined by her own satisfactions.

Another type of ambivalent mother is the woman who has never accepted the feminine role. She feels humiliated in being a woman, is envious of men, and lacks the "nest-making" tendencies. Her marriage relationship is conflictual, and she finds the process of pregnancy and childbirth distasteful. She may have become pregnant by accident, or to please her husband, or to prove that she can function as a woman. Pregnancy may interfere with her career and by impairing her physical attractiveness give her a depreciated feeling. A mother who tends to feel very guilty about her rejective feelings for her child will often over-compensate by exact, meticulous care of him.

As the child's response toward food is largely determined by his feelings toward the person who feeds him, his feeding behavior becomes expressive of these attitudes. Refusal of food may be his retaliation. His mother does not gratify his emotional needs; he, in turn, will not please her by doing what she requests of him.

Some of the most extreme cases of food rejection occur in children who have been totally abandoned by their mothers and for whom no substitute mother is available.

In varying degrees of severity an infant's disturbance in nursing behavior reflects his dissatisfaction with the degree of tender loving care which he receives. He may react with gastrointestinal disturbances, such as vomiting, colic, or rumination. Such a baby does not gain weight as he should and may be tried on various formulas without success until it is realized that it is the way he is treated and fed, rather than what he is fed that makes the difference.

A striking condition found in older infants is rumination. The ruminating infant regurgitates food he has previously swallowed and rechews and reswallows it only to repeat the process. The child seems preoccupied with rumination. In the process of regurgitation and reswallowing, a considerable amount of food may be lost and nutritional problems may develop. Rumination is frequently mistaken for a condition of organic rather than psychologic origin. It is found in infants with a severely disturbed maternal relationship. The infant, lacking gratification ordinarily derived from his mother, turns his attention toward himself and toward the food he has ingested, seeking gratification from its manipulation. The child with rumination ordinarily responds promptly, and often dramatically, to the establishment of a satisfactory maternal relationship — often with a substitute maternal figure. As the symptoms disappear, the nutritional problems are alleviated. Treatment on a pediatric ward in a hospital is often required for the acute phase of management.

Other infants express their dissatisfaction by demanding frequent feeding and seeming always hungry, though their intake is sufficient for good nourishment. Others seem apathetic and tend to fall asleep during nursing. There is no enthusiasm in their approach to the breast or bottle.

A traumatic weaning experience may condition to unfavorable attitudes toward feeding.[1] Change from the breast or bottle to the cup means loss of sucking satisfaction and a change in the interpersonal aspects of feeding. This seems to be tolerated earlier and more abruptly by some babies than by others. The relinquishing of any pattern of feeding constitutes weaning. Giving up the breast, the bottle, and the night bottle are examples of this. If such a process occurs gradually, at a time when the child has substitute gratifications available and when the child is emotionally ready, then weaning need not be traumatic. A weaning process which the child is able to accept is a growth experience which helps him to prepare for the loss of sources of gratification in later life. In contrast, an abrupt weaning process for which the child is unprepared may produce frustrations beyond the adaptive capacity of the child. Under such circumstances the opposite of growth and mastery, namely symptom formation, may occur. Such neurotic defensive adaptive mechanisms are incorporated into the character just as the healthy adaptive mechanisms of growth are incorporated.

Under conditions of stress, as the birth of a sibling, it is common for a child to return to feeding patterns, such as the bottle or night bottle, which may have been previously given up.

[1] Spock and Huschka: Psychological Aspects of Pediatric Practice. In Blumer, G: *Practitioners' Library of Medicine and Surgery*, Vol. 13, 1957.

This is an example of regression to the adaptive patterns of a previous developmental period in response to a stress stimulus. This is a characteristic human response and we shall see many illustrations of it later.

Unfortunately, the timing of weaning may be determined by circumstances extraneous to the child's needs. It may be necessitated by illness of the mother or her return to work; thus, the baby is coincidentally deprived of his mother's presence and of his source of oral gratification. It may occur when the mother becomes pregnant again and, if the pregnancy is unacceptable to her, her unstable mood may affect her child. Weaning may be initiated by the mother to conform to training-time tales of her friends.

The mother's attitude during the weaning period is of much significance in setting up conditioned patterns of behavior. Love and affection from her and encouragement of the child in his new techniques help him to accept the new situation. If, however, she shames or frightens him into giving up the nipple and tends to withdraw from him during the weaning period, she creates in him an unfavorable mental set, one expression of which may be a rebellious attitude toward eating.

Family attitudes also influence the child during his early attempts to feed himself. Strong disapproval of messiness may lead the mother or father to put food into the child's mouth rather than encourage him to do it himself. This keeps him in a passive attitude and may intimidate him to such an extent as to interfere with his enjoyment of his meal.

The young child often plays a feeding game for the attention of his mother. By a disinterest in food he expresses his dissatisfaction with her and, at the same time, arouses her anxiety and increased attention. This is a way of asserting himself as free of her, even while he demands her concern. The mother plays into the game with threats and bribery, and it often becomes a contest of wills.

The child whose mother is overly anxious about him may develop feeding problems not so much in retaliation against her as in protest against the tense and dutiful feelings associated with meals. The mother's — or father's — compulsiveness makes mealtime unpleasant for the child. Choice of foods is determined not by taste but by "what is good for you." This type of feeding problem is common among middle and upper class families in which food is plentiful and there is much attention to the correct balancing of meals. The child is allowed little choice and is often coaxed or bullied into eating the "good for you" foods, before he is allowed to have something he likes.

A four-year-old girl, A. L., was brought to the clinic because she refused to eat all solid food. The history indicated that the family was in great emotional turmoil. The father had lost his job and the mother's attitude was quite depressed. For the past several months the child had got little attention from either parent. Immediately on hospitalization the child began to eat solid foods, but as soon as she was returned home she again stopped eating. Hospitalization the second time was more prolonged, and during the period of hospitalization the parents were given an understanding of the child's problem. Upon return home, following this hospitalization, the child did not stop eating solid food and the parents were encouraged not to pay too much attention to the eating problem, but to give the child a good deal of attention in other ways.

It is interesting in this connection to mention the study of Dr. Clara M. Davis[1] of the feeding habits of young children allowed to select their own food. Dr. Davis found that, over a period of time, young children allowed to select freely from a variety of foods would balance their diets.

The child's attitudes toward food may, of course, be affected by people other than his mother. A father's fussy or dominating behavior may make mealtime conflictual. Arguments at the table, teasing by siblings, over-solicitous grandparents, are all possible etiologic factors in the development of a feeding problem. The dinner hour in many families is not a time of relaxed, pleasant being-together. Father is tired or remote and irritable, the mother harassed and the children quarrelsome. The young child's impressions of food are negatively influenced by such an atmosphere. Breakfast is also often a hurried, anxious time. Older

[1]Davis, Clara M.: Self selection of diet by newly weaned infants. *Am. J. Dis. Child.*, 36: 1928.

children, particularly, may be worried about the school day ahead to such a degree as to refuse breakfast or even to develop nausea and vomiting at that time. For reasons not always obvious, some children as well as adults prefer certain meals to others and their attitude should, in most cases, be taken into account. Forcing a large breakfast or lunch, for example, on a child who has no interest in food at that time can intensify the problem.

Specific food resistances and cravings may indicate, for example, a need for salt. The study of Dr. Davis, previously mentioned, illustrates the average child's innate capacity, over the long run, to select according to his physiologic needs.

There are, however, many psychogenic determinants for specific food choice. Too rapid forcing of a new food may prejudice the baby or young child against it. As has already been observed, too much stress upon foods that are presumably good for the child, creates an unpleasant association. Some children remain overly dependent on milk and refuse most solid foods. This may be aggravated by a too aggressive attempt to force these foods. On the other hand, it may be allowed to persist because the mother lacks time and/or interest patiently to condition the child to an acceptance of solids.

Specific foods may be associated with a variety of frightening or disgusting experiences. The ill child who vomits his carrots, for instance, may retain a dislike for this vegetable. The shape or color of food may have unpleasant conditioning. The child may have observed a real or imaginary bug or hair in a bowl of cereal, developing thereafter a distaste for this food or for all foods served in this bowl.

So strong is the tendency to identify feelings for food with feelings for people that "tastes" are determined to a large extent by such associations. A father or mother dislikes fish or eats only the white meat of chicken; the children sometimes take over this prejudice. If, on the other hand, a disliked or feared person shows particular interest in a food item this may be refused by the child. For example, a five-year-old girl who had previously liked tomatoes suddenly developed a revulsion for them. It was discovered that she had often been given tomatoes by a neighbor who had an ulcerating carcinoma of his face. After the child had seen the uncovered lesions, she no longer would eat tomatoes.

We have observed that the infant and the young child seek oral gratification and that the sucking experience involving stimulation of lips and mouth is important to him. As soon as his motor coordination allows, he gets his finger, hand, or thumb into his mouth. The satisfaction obtained in this way exists apart from the process of nourishment and may be especially utilized when the child is tired or seems restless or lonely. This "orality" which is so obvious in the early months of life is an expression of the dependent incorporative character of that period. The baby is a "taking" creature; his first interest in the world is determined by the satisfaction of his biological needs. But, as we have seen, these needs are from the beginning not limited to food intake. He needs to be given love and stimulation and interest; he must be taught and encouraged and guided. At the same time he must, of course, be led gradually to control and modify his demands on those around him and to find satisfaction in giving as well as taking. Extreme attitudes on the part of the parents, in the direction of either deprivation or pampering, may favor the child's persistence in infantile attitudes expressed in the development of a character structure with strong oral orientation.

A person of this character type has emotionally greedy attitudes. He needs excessive reassurance and love. He feels the lack of inner resources and must depend on others to nourish him with support, praise and affection. He does not give easily or does so only in hope of reward. Such a person is predisposed to difficulty in interpersonal relations because his friends may sense the insatiable nature of his demands on them. Rejection increases his orality, and a vicious circle is set up which may lead to a more or less severe character distortion.

It has often been noted in the treatment of psychiatric patients that oral fixations are correlated with experiences of deprivation in early life. Some patients have a history of infantile feeding difficulties, with malnourishment related to unsatisfactory breast milk or formula. More frequently the deprivation has been psychological. The emotionally deprived child may develop into the "hungry" adult who all his life demands and seeks tender loving care. To be sure, the oral needs of some individuals seem to be constitutionally stronger than those of others and there is a good deal of variation in tolerance of deprivation. But there is a necessary minimum of gratification which every child must receive if he is to develop into a mature, socially integrated adult.

Pampering may, of course, be overdone and parents, by excessive concern to satisfy the child's every wish, may tempt him to remain in a situation of infantile orality. Self satisfaction must be associated with consideration for others, and the developing child needs to be encouraged to learn the pleasure of giving as well as taking.

We have seen food rejection resulting from inadequate emotional gratification. In some cases, however, a symptom develops in the opposite direction, and a child becomes an over-eater. The obese child, too, has a feeding problem. He may eat because his mother urges him to do so and he reacts in a docile, passive way to hold her affection, or he may eat greedily as though attempting in this way to compensate for lack of other satisfactions. This problem will be examined more fully later as we discuss the subject of obesity.

A condition characterized by indiscriminate and insatiable ingestion of material, edible or otherwise, is known in pediatric practice as "pica." No physiologic cause for this perverse behavior has been found, and it seems to represent an intense oral craving.

Pica is most commonly found in children two or three years of age. It tends to disappear spontaneously. The occurrence of pica at this age may or may not be an indication of psychological disturbance. However, the continued ingestion of inedible material and objects may have dangerous consequences. In many older buildings in large cities there may be many layers of old paint on the walls. The commercial paint preparations used in past years had high concentrations of lead. Such old paint tends to peel and fall to the floor, thus becoming available for ingestion by the child with pica. The continued ingestion of such paint leads to the development of lead poisoning with severe encephalopathy and possible death. Severely afflicted children who recover may be left with partial paralysis, loss of intellectual powers, and emotional instability.

Pica may illustrate the manner in which an emotional problem of relatively mild or moderate degree may become a major threat to an individual by leading to the ingestion of harmful materials.

Pica in older children represents a more severe disturbance of behavior. It is usually associated with a marked emotional disturbance in the child and a marked degree of intrafamilial disturbance. It is a general principle that symptoms in childhood must be understood and evaluated within the context of the age and maturational level of the child.

A boy aged seven, R. T., was brought to the hospital with the report that he wandered over the neighborhood and ate out of garbage cans. The father reported that the mother had not been out of the house in seven years. She had suffered a postpartum psychosis after the birth of this child and had been seriously disturbed for the first three years of his life. She was still depressed and withdrawn. The father admitted that he had been having an affair with another woman and that he had little interest in the home. The mother served meals out of cans and occasionally the older daughter attempted to cook a meal. The boy, even after having been fed, would go out every day and eat garbage out of the cans in the neighborhood. In this case, the home was so pathologic that it was felt necessary to place the child in a foster home, in addition to undertaking a program of intensive psychotherapy. The child remained rather withdrawn but discontinued eating out of garbage cans.

A conditioning to rejection or excessive intake or specific fussiness about food does not necessarily terminate with childhood. Obesity, the condition of excessive appetite known as "bulemia" or the aversion to food known as "anorexia nervosa," all indicate the persistence of unfavorable infantile attitudes in adult life.

We have described the infant as an oral being whose primary need is to be fed physically and psychically. He does best in an environment which satisfies his innate needs for nourishment, for stimulation and for love. His feeding behavior is closely related to the degree of satisfaction of these needs.

It is obvious, too, that the child is not merely passively needful, but that he is self-asserting, demanding and resistive in response to the treatment he receives. As we study the next phase of development, we will see more clearly the role of the aggressive drives in character formation. At this point, we may only point out the relationship between feeding behavior and aggressive strivings. Biting and anger are closely related in the animal kingdom and the concept of "gnashing of teeth" as an expression of rage indicates that this relationship exists in human beings, though less obviously than in the lower animals.

As the baby becomes possessed of teeth, he bites and chews the objects he puts into his mouth. To a large extent, this represents a stimulation of the gums and a biologic tendency to use a newly developed function. It may, however, become correlated with aggressive feelings and the child may bite in anger. Such behavior is quickly frowned upon and punished so that it is subject to early repression. Severe repression of strong biting impulses may involve even the biting of food so that the child tends to avoid solid foods, especially meat, and to prefer milk and very soft materials. To understand this we should understand the meaning and purpose of the phenomenon of repression.

Very early every individual begins to formulate an awareness of behavior and attitudes which are acceptable. At first his standards are those of his parents or parent substitutes. They approve or disapprove, reward or punish, and the child conforms to this external code. As he identifies his outlook with that prevailing around him he makes this code a part of himself. Conformity for the sake of avoiding the disapproval of others continues, but added to this is the need to avoid disapproval of one's self. We say the child is developing a superego or social personality component. (This will be discussed in detail later.) As we observe the child, even in his first year, we see indications of his social development in his expressions of guilt and shame. He is developing a concept of himself as a social being. Impulses or even thoughts that do not fit into this concept tend to be consciously inhibited; that is, suppressed. As time goes on, suppression becomes automatic and proceeds without conscious awareness. This process of automatic inhibition of unacceptable impulses and the thoughts and feelings associated with them we call "repression." It is an economical maneuver by which the human being avoids having constantly to pass judgment on himself. One does not have to stop in every situation of frustration to decide whether to scream or strike or run. One automatically behaves according to his concept of how he should behave.

Repression is obviously normal and universal. It can, however, lead to difficulty. The individual whose biological needs are excessively repressed and who is forced by parent figures into a pattern of behavior which does not allow sufficient self expression and assertion, functions in precarious equilibrium. The repressed strivings are not eliminated and may threaten from time to time to break through. Often they do break through in some distorted ways, many of which we will observe later. If not, they necessitate rigid controls which constitute handicaps to personality development.

Biting serves simultaneously for feeding and as a potential means of destruction. The child, as he becomes aware of this potentiality, may be frightened by it. This, therefore, is an area in which he early becomes inhibited, not only because of external regulations but also because of his own guilt. In other words, he feels both external and internal pressures to control his biting impulses.

The child whose biting impulses have become associated with anger and have been subjected to severe internal and external repression often is so rigidly inhibited in this function that he represses all his biting impulses. The inhibition has spread out indiscriminately. This process of diffusion and displacement of inhibition will be seen frequently as the basis for psychiatric symptoms. Here, it is of interest as one possible cause of difficulty in the child who develops a disinclination for solid foods. The repression may be excessive either because the child's aggression is overly stimulated or because he is greatly intimidated. The inhibition may have been conditioned by specific experiences, such as seeing animals bite. Biting and consuming have become associated in some extreme cases with the powerful taboo on cannibalism, so that eating becomes frightening and guilt-provoking.

A nine-year-old boy, T. P., was brought for psychiatric consultation because he had suddenly refused to eat meat of any kind. This began after he had read a newspaper report about a man who had been discovered to be murdering his neighbors and eating parts of their bodies.

The boy's history indicated that he had always had various food idiosyncracies. His mother and grandmother had both devoted much time to feeding him. His grandmother followed Kosher rules and his mother pretended to do so, but secretly slipped the boy such items as ham and bacon. His father also gave lip service to Kosher but made exceptions. This child was the oldest of three. It was said that when his sister, three years younger, was born he became very much upset and at times would bite this sister. His kindergarten teacher reported also that T. P. bit the other children at school. The child had been abruptly weaned from the bottle at the age of one year. The parents admitted that they favored the younger children, but said this boy was the grandmother's favorite. It was believed that his identification with the grandmother's Kosher taboos, his hostility toward his parents and siblings, and his fear of his own aggression all provided the background for his reaction to this story of frank cannibalism.

The child's resistive, rebellious attitudes may be mobilized during the period of toilet training. At this time he is being trained to behave not only according to prescribed rules but also to assume an imposed attitude. Feces must be regarded as dirty, and soiling as bad. The rebellious attitudes, as well as the concept of dirtiness, may affect the child's feeding behavior. If he is being subjected to strong pressure to control his habits of elimination, he may express his aggression in other ways. Food resistance and fussiness may be one such expression. If he cannot eliminate to suit himself, he will eat to suit himself!

The feelings of disgust which parents somewhat deliberately cultivate during the training period may be subject to a diffusion such as we have previously observed in relation to biting. Not only feces are disgusting but so are all brown substances or mushy substances, and the child consequently refuses to eat foods that have, in his mind, any such similarity. He may become excessively preoccupied with the idea of dirt and suspicious of any substances, such as raisins or nuts, in his food.

It is therefore not uncommon for a child who has previously

been eating well to develop food fussiness while he is being toilet trained. The correct approach to this problem is, of course, correlated with the parents' attitude toward training. The feeding symptom is but one small expression of the child's "anal" conflict. This subject will be discussed in a later chapter.

As the child's sexual curiosities and fantasies develop, his sexual concepts may involve orality. The idea of a baby "in mother's stomach" combined with the vague concept of its having been put there by father, can add up to a concept of oral impregnation. Food becomes subject to sexual taboo. Such fantasies have been revealed by children who have developed the extreme symptom of revulsion for food known as anorexia nervosa. This occurs most often in pubescent girls but has been described in younger children and, occasionally, in boys and it may also occur in adult women.[*]

There is a primitive character to the oral sexual fantasies of severely disturbed children which reminds us of the tendency in primitive cultures to stress fasting and sexual abstinence as purification procedures and, on the contrary, to indulge at other times in orgies of feasting and sexual gratification. Both represent indulgence of the flesh as opposed to the spiritual life.

The first experiences of life center around the feeding experience. Adaptive patterns developed at this level subsequently become the basis for patterns of adjustment. As has been indicated, traumatic experiences at this early, vulnerable period of life may make the child unprepared for the stress of further developmental periods. This may be reflected in psychopathologic responses both in later childhood and adult life.

SUMMARY

The child's feeding needs begin with adequate nourishment. The amount and frequency of the food needed varies with different children, and it also varies in the individual, from time to time, depending on his health and growth period. A degree of scheduling of the feeding period tends to stabilize most infants,

---

[*]Wall, J. H.: Anorexia Nervosa. Bulletin N.Y. Academy Medicine 32:116 (1956).

but this should be based, as much as possible, on the appetite cycle and adjusted from time to time as that cycle varies.

Inasmuch as the feeding periods bring the child into his first and closest attachment to another person, usually the mother, the interaction of child and mother during these periods is of great importance in determining not only his attitude toward food but also his concept of himself in relation to other people. Severe problems of feeding, when not physiologically determined, are, therefore, a reflection of dissatisfaction and conflict in interpersonal relationships.

The mother's attitudes toward her child are determined by many factors, some of which are transparent and relatively superficial and some indicative of her basic difficulty in accepting a mature feminine role. Negative attitudes may be expressed in ways of overt rejection or may be over-compensated for by meticulous concern or may reveal themselves in inconsistent, tense behavior. The child responds sensitively to such attitudes, although some children can tolerate more emotional deprivation than others.

The child with a feeding problem may be acting out retaliation against the mother, contesting his will against hers, making excessive demands on her or withdrawing from her in apathetic disinterest. Lacking adequate emotional stimulus and gratification in this early period, he may carry over into adult life an oral attitude of "emotional greediness" which predisposes him to maladjustment.

The parents' approach to weaning, self-feeding and food choice, affects the infant's feeding pattern. Specific idiosyncracies may indicate unpleasant associations or connotations of the particular food. The act of biting may, in some children, be associated with anger and aggression so rigidly repressed as to interfere with enjoyment of solid foods. During the training period, the resistiveness aroused by parental discipline may aggravate the feeding problem.

It is obvious that the personality of the child begins to take form during the earliest months of life and that it is influenced to a large extent by the mother-child interactions associated with feeding.

SUGGESTED READINGS

Aldrich, C. A., and Aldrich, M. M.: *Feeding our Old-fashioned Children.* New York, Macmillan, 1942.

Bliss, E. L., and Branch, C. H.: *Anorexia Nervosa.* New York, Paul B. Hoeber, Inc., 1960.

Bowlby, J.: The nature of the child's tie to his mother. *Int. J. Psychoanalysis, 39:*350, 1958.

Finch, S. M.: *Fundamentals of Child Psychiatry.* New York, W. W. Norton, 1960.

Hoch, P., and Zubin, Jr. (Eds.): *Psychopathology of Childhood.* New York, Grune & Stratton, 1955.

Escalona, S.: Emotional Development in the First Year of Life, in *Problems of Infancy and Childhood,* edited by Senn, M. E., New York, Josiah Macy Foundation, 1954.

Levy, D.: *Maternal Overprotection.* New York, Columbia University Press, 1943.

La Leche International: *The Womanly Art of Breast Feeding.* Franklin Park, Illinois, 1963.

Lurie, O.: Psychological factors associated with eating difficulties in children, *Am. J. Orthopsych. II:*452, 1941.

Montague, A.: *Constitutional and Prenatal Factors in Infant and Child Health.* New York, Josiah Macy, Jr., Foundation, 1950.

Richmond, J. B., Eddy, E. J., and Green, M.: Rumination. Pediatrics, 22:49, 1958.

Wolf, K. M.: Observations of Individual Tendencies in the First Year of Life, in *Problems of Infancy and Childhood.* Edited by Senn, M. E., New York, Josiah Macy Foundation, 1954.

Wolf, K. M.: Problems of early infancy, *J. Am. Psychoanalytic Ass'n,* 3:506, 1955.

Chapter III

Aggression and Character Disorders

WE HAVE noted that the human infant needs, for optimal growth and development, not only adequate food but also personal attention, stimulation and love. We have seen that his incorporative needs soon become affected by his interactions with the people who feed him, so that many feeding problems reflect unsatisfactory interpersonal relationships.

The infant, however, is not merely incorporative nor merely passively receptive. He needs to receive but he needs also to manipulate, to express himself, to rebel against domination. Each person is born with this potentiality for aggression. Screaming, kicking, resisting and attacking are normally observed in childhood. Children vary greatly as to the violence of these aggressive activities, depending on the constitution and the severity of frustration to which they are exposed. Aggressiveness of some degree, however, is universal. The methods the child develops for expression or control of his aggression determine, to a large extent, his character structure as an adult.

Although everyone agrees that potential for aggression is to be found in all normal individuals, there are differences of interpretation as to the genesis and purpose of aggression. In his early work Sigmund Freud[1] defines it as primordial hostile reaction to frustration. This implies that aggression does not originate solely as a derivative of the biologic need for discharge of tension. Aggression in its development, according to Freud, involves destructive and hostile elements which are counterbalanced by constructive and life-preserving components.

Some psychoanalysts, particularly Melanie Klein[2] and her followers, stress the significance of destructive impulses in the

---

[1]Freud, Sigmund: *Complete Works*. Vol. XX, Chap. VII. London, Hogarth Press, 1959.

[2]Klein, Melanie: *Am. J. Psychology*, 105:241.

very young infant. They interpret the child's aggressive approach to his mother as having a consuming quality which may be a basis for guilt and depression in him with consequent symptom formation. Followers of Klein feel that the child's efforts to deal with the feelings aroused by his aggression form the basis for much subsequent psychopathology.

Such negative definitions, however, under-emphasize the fact that aggression may have constructive elements and be an expression of the child's need to master and to learn rather than only to destroy. Thus, a child may pull his toy apart because of curiosity rather than because of anger. Loretta Bender[3] feels that we may define destructive aggression as that which threatens the well-being of other people. Other types of aggression may be directed toward experimentation, exploration and control. Hendricks[1] and Schilder[2] both emphasize the human tendency to seize and control, to learn, as expressed in aggressive activities.

The infant or child needs a reasonable degree of freedom to express his developing interests. He must expend his excess energy in exploratory activity. This is not necessarily destructive or hostile in intent even though it may at times threaten the established order about the child. When, however, normal exploratory activities are excessively suppressed, the child reacts with anger. He may express this in defiant action or in temper tantrums, in which case he is described as an aggressive child. He may, however, express his rage in the form of passive resistance. Often when there is interference with the child's striving for mastery and self expression, he responds with behavior which seems to represent a kind of disorganization, and his energies waste themselves in restless, undirected activity.

We may, therefore, see aggression as a representation of the conflict between the natural strivings for self expression and the suppressive forces of the environment. Aggressive behavior may be active or passive, constructive or destructive, patterned or disorganized. The forms which it assumes are determined by the

---

[3]Bender, Loretta: *Aggression, Hostility and Anxiety in Children.* Springfield, Thomas, 1953.
[1]Hendricks, I.: *Psychoanalytic Quart.*, II:33.
[2]Schilder, P.: *Goals and Desires of Man.* Columbia Univ. Press, 1949.

interaction between the individual with his adaptive potentialities and the nature of the impacts of his environment.

The child, as later the adult, fights for autonomy. He struggles against passivity, against domination. To submit without protest to the demands of the world is to feel overwhelmed, helpless, defeated. On the other hand, the child accomplishes nothing by undirected destructive action, by protest for the sake of protest. These two extremes of reaction may be illustrated by two extremes of infant behavior.

> An institutional baby, A. C., had spent all of his eighteen months of life in a large institution where he got little individual attention. He sat passively in his crib or when placed out on the floor sat or walked about aimlessly. He seldom cried and rarely reached out for a toy or other objects around him though his facial expression indicated interest in them. During painful medical manipulation he whimpered softly but did not resist. He sometimes "talked to himself," indicating a vocabulary consistent with his age, but he rarely initiated verbal communication.

Excessive frustration and deprivation favor the development of unhealthy patterns of aggression. Similar behavior may, however, result when the parents over-indulge and "spoil" the child. Parental attitudes which impose no restraints are often an over-compensation for rejection. The mother's need constantly to deny her own angry and resentful feelings toward her child makes it difficult for her to discipline him. As a result, the child's behavior is influenced in large measure by his restless seeking for gratification. He does not learn to postpone the immediate satisfaction of his needs and gradually to develop ways of social adaptation. He lacks a recognition of strength or consistency in his parents. His diffusely aggressive behavior brings him little satisfaction. In those cases where the pampering is motivated by rejection and guilt, the child is often sensitive to the mother's conflictual feelings about him, and his aggressive behavior is intensified by retaliatory feelings.

> A. N., an eight-year-old boy, the son of professional parents, was brought into the clinic because of destructiveness at school. He is reported to have hit children, to have been intolerant of

competition and to be prone to temper tantrums. The beginning of his acting-out behavior is dated to the time he was two and a half years old, when his sibling was born. He is said to have bit her, to have regressed to anorexia at that time and to have shown extreme jealousy of the sister. He was entered in a progressive nursery school when he was four, but was rejected there after three months because he was said to have no control of his behavior.

His parents argued a great deal about discipline of the child. The mother believed in extreme permissiveness, stating that she did not want to impose any restriction on his creativity. The father felt otherwise but was unable to enforce his point of view, particularly since all four of the grandparents agreed with the wife. As a result, the father "gave up" on the boy and turned his attention to the daughter.

The history of the mother indicated that she had been very jealous of her own brother and had often said that she had wanted to be a boy. Her extreme permissiveness was seen by the psychiatrists as a compensation for rejection of her son. After his birth, she had continued with her career and had spent little time with her children. She stated that she was unable to say no to the boy and had a very guilty feeling if she ever did. If she did try to be restrictive of him he managed to manipulate his grandparents to get his own way. As the father withdrew, the mother became more involved with the child.

Initially, it seemed as though treatment was impossible because the mother regarded the child's behavior as "cute," and encouraged him in it. She refused treatment for herself. However, later, after a critical situation developed at school she accepted the idea of treatment, as did the father.

The therapist encouraged the mother to spend more time with the children but to be firm in disciplining them. The father was urged to take over a great deal of control. It was soon observed that the boy felt much more comfortable under these circumstances and his behavior indicated a good deal of improvement.

In contrast to this, was the history of an overly repressed child who came from a firmly authoritative and patriarchal family. The father and his father before him were very con-

trolling and rigid people. He expressed a wish for his son to
be "a real man" and felt that the way to achieve this real man-
hood in his son was to expose the child to hardships and frustrations. The boy, however, was a weak and frail child with
interest in art of which his father was ashamed.

The child was brought to the clinic when he was thirteen,
following a change in his personality. He had become aggressive and destructive, no longer submissive to his father's discipline. The father reacted in an ambivalent way. He was
pleased to see his son express himself, yet he was very punitive
with the boy when he disobeyed him.

The mother was a masochistic woman — a good wife according to family standards.

The father refused to change his attitude, and tried to
manipulate the therapist to follow his instructions in dealing
with the boy. It was obvious that the boy, though very rebellious, was extremely frightened of his destructive impulses.
He had violent dreams of world conflagration and the like. It
was felt that he was developing potentially antisocial behavior
with a good deal of sexually sadistic fantasy. However, in view
of the fact that the family completely refused treatment it was
felt that there was nothing which the clinic could do for him.

The pediatrician or psychiatrist presented with an aggressively over-active patient must consider the possibility that this
is a brain-damaged child. Loretta Bender[1] says "The sadistic
impulses of children are closely related to the primitiveness of
their motor impulses and the degree of hyperactivity. * * * *
Accordingly, in clinical practice, it is sometimes difficult to
differentiate between a sadism derived from environmental
(psychological) factors and one which reaches deep down into
organic layers."

The reaction of the brain-damaged child is described as a
diffuse kind of hyperactivity with distractability, over-response
to stimuli, refractoriness to control. Goldstein[2] speaks of the

---

[1]Bender, Loretta: *Aggression, Hostility and Anxiety in Children.* Springfield,
Thomas, 1953.
Also Bender, L.: In Modern Trends in Child Psychiatry. Pacella and Lewis,
Editors. New York, International Universities Press, 1945.
[2]Goldstein, K.: *Psychiatry, 15*:245, 1952.

tendency to "catastrophic reactions" in some brain-damaged children. The acting-out tends to be less clearly related to any specific situation than does that of the psychogenically aggressive child. In some organic brain disease there is a deficiency in the ability to control reactions directed toward gratification of immediate needs. It is, however, often difficult, in the absence of any objective evidences of central nervous system damage, to differentiate the two etiologic groups. The history of difficult delivery, with a possible period of anoxia, or of the occurrence of illness in infancy with encephalitic features or convulsions, would favor an organic diagnosis. There may, of course, be an abnormality of the central nervous system without obvious objective signs of neurologic malfunctioning and with no history of cerebral damage. Diagnosis depends on a careful study of the child's behavior, careful neurologic examination and on psychologic tests analyzed against the background of the child's social environment.

The value of psychological tests in the detection of the brain-damaged older child and adult has been appreciated for many years. More recently there has been considerable interest in the use of developmental tests for the diagnosis of brain injury in the infant and younger child. The development of testing methods was dependent upon the establishment of standardized developmental norms in infants and young children. Much of this work was done by Gesell and coworkers. Although every pediatrician uses developmental norms for diagnosis, greater accuracy and reproducibility can be attained by the adoption of formal testing methods. Such methods include the Stanford-Binet and the Wechsler intelligence tests as well as the Rorschach and other projective tests.

It is possible by these tests to detect not only grossly abnormal infants but also others with more modest defects. In some instances infants who demonstrate retardation by these tests, as a result of such conditions as a recent central nervous system infection or hypothyroidism, may recover and subsequently show normal development. Developmental tests are of greater value after the age of four months, although neurologic abnormalities in grossly damaged infants can be detected earlier. It is, of course, evident that normal development in infancy does not preclude subsequent retardation caused by infection, degenerative disease or injury. In the school-age child psychological testing may give material of great validity and predictive value with regard to intelligence and personality structure.

Proper testing of infants and young children utilizes motor, adaptive, linguistic and personal-social parameters for diagnosis. Adaptive behavior is the most important measure of moderate retardation. Although these tests in infancy can detect retardation and brain damage with great accuracy, they are of little value in predicting the intelligence level eventually achieved by infants who have no neurologic handicap. Developmental tests reflect only crudely those factors of a psychosocial nature within the family setting which stimulate the development of intelligence. The more widespread use of developmental diagnosis may lead to the detection in infancy of individuals with organic brain involvement. Correct diagnosis is worth while because of the secondary importance of an intensive exploration of the personal relationships of the brain-damaged child. On the other hand, such a study is of primary importance in arriving at an understanding of the psychogenically aggressive child. Many children present coexistent organic disease and functional disorders, especially since the child with organic pathology routinely provokes interpersonal psychopathology in the family due to the management problem. The presence of organic pathology does not necessarily mean that therapy for the functional component may not be useful.

A boy, aged 14, was seen by a psychiatrist because of personality changes following an automobile accident. He had incurred multiple fractures, including a skull fracture, and had been in coma for five weeks following the accident.

The history indicated that the boy had previously made a good school and social adjustment. After emerging from the comatose state he showed restless irritable behavior and became a hospital management problem. His behavior was sexually uninhibited and destructive and he rebelled violently at any controls. A psychometric test made several months after the accident showed a drop of 15 points below his previous intelligence quotient. It was finally necessary, because of his destructive behavior, to transfer him to a psychiatric hospital.

The organic factor in this case is clear, but the boy's behavior did not differ greatly from that observed in some children with no such history and in whom the aggressive-destructive attitude seems definitely related to psychic rather than to organic trauma.

A deviant pattern of social behavior is most commonly the result of the conditioning impact on a normal individual of destructive and confusing interpersonal experiences. If these damaging experiences occur in early life they may create a basically hostile and defensive attitude toward people which, in some cases, is as difficult to modify as though it were caused by organic brain damage.

Anna Freud says, in *War and Children,* "It is one of the recognized aims of education to deal with the aggressiveness of the child's nature; that is, in the course of the first four or five years to change the child's own attitude toward these impulses in himself. They are usually first restricted, a little later repressed."

The parent and educator must be aware of their responsibilities to help the child to deal constructively with his aggressive impulses.

The patterning of the child's innate potentialities proceeds in close relationship to his superego development. By superego[1] is meant the social-moral component of personality. It is that complex of standards, codes, self-demands, which becomes part of oneself and modifies one's primitive drives into accordance with the expectations of his social milieu.

Conformity and self-control in the very young child is at first clearly related to his recognition of rewards and punishments. It is externally determined. The good child is loved and rewarded; the bad child is disapproved and punished. He acts accordingly. It can be observed, however, that at a very early age the child shows evidence of a sense of guilt and shame in relation to socially disapproved behavior. From this time on, he is motivated not only by what the world demands of him but, also, by what he demands of himself. This incorporation

[1]Freud, S.: *The Ego and the Id.* London, Hogarth Press, 1927.

of the social standards results in the formation of an internal self-critical function that is called superego. Superego functions to a large extent unconsciously: a fact which explains much of the self-destructive and self-limiting activity which occurs frequently in psychopathology.

The character of any person's superego, reflecting as it does the mores to which he has been exposed, is to a large extent environmentally conditioned. We grant that the constitutional temperament of the child influences his ease or difficulty in accepting social codes, his capacity for control, and his ability to perceive and accept the needs of other people. But granting this, we still can most constructively approach problems involving superego if we study them as arising out of the struggles of the child to modify his primitive impulses in such a way as to win approval and avoid punishment in his particular kind of environment.

The parents' effect on the child is, of course, of primary importance and the parents' attitudes are, in turn, influenced by their own families and by the traditions of their culture. Some social groups allow, or even encourage as morally justified, acts of aggression which in other groups would be disapproved. The child very early observes the behavior of those around him and senses what is expected of him. His response depends, to a large extent, on the manner in which the expectations are presented. Dominating, rigid parents who intimidate the child and severely disapprove any aggressive activity necessitate much repression on his part. His own angry and destructive attitudes become too dangerous to face; they must be kept unconscious and their existence denied even to himself. Such conditioning results in the development of a formalistic kind of superego. Conformity is effected by a fear of retaliation. The moral principles are not valued nor really believed in though they may be scrupulously followed. The child with a superego of this kind may be compulsively docile but his hostility will express itself in disguised ways directed either against others or against himself. He may fail in his school work — though intellectually bright — and in that way express his resentment. His sense of guilt about his own aggressive impulses may be so intense as to express itself in self-destructive ways as, for example, accident proneness. The tension involved in the severe repression may be evident in such symptoms as tics or stammering. A great variety of behavior disorders may result from the operation of a formalistic, severe superego.

Superego formation proceeds more favorably in the child whose moral attitudes result, not from categorical repression, but from a kind of identification with adults whom he loves and respects. Such a process of identification is largely unconscious though the child at times overtly recognizes and expresses the fact that he wants to be "like mother" or "like daddy." As a gradual process over the developmental years, he takes over their codes as he does their mannerisms without awareness of doing so. He no longer says, "Mother doesn't want us to put muddy shoes on the chair," instead he says, "We don't put muddy shoes on the chair."

The expression on a child's face as he watches another child misbehave is often a fascinating study in ambivalence. The child with a well developed superego will indicate disapproval, sometimes with a suggestion of anxiety, sometimes of glee at the thought that the child may be punished. In other cases, the expression vacillates between vicarious enjoyment of the misbehavior and smug or anxious attitudes about it.

The three to five-year-old child, in the process of developing a stable relationship to the total family constellation, goes through a series of experiences called the Oedipal neurosis, which will be described later. Part of this process of development as a social being involves a structuring and reinforcing of superego.

Children are sensitive to hypocrisy and often show good awareness of the fact that their parents teach them to behave according to rules which they themselves do not follow. Self-controlled and socially considerate behavior develops more readily as a result of example, than as a result of preaching. Consistency of example, too, is important. It is difficult for a child to comprehend the meaning of social restrictions when at times he is allowed to act in a certain way and at other times is punished for such behavior. Under such circumstances he tends to constantly test out, to see what he can "get by with."

It has already been mentioned that toilet training may represent to the child a kind of power struggle with the parents and may therefore bring out in him a good deal of active or passive aggression. The issue here is conformity of behavior. To this there become attached moralistic attitudes concerning cleanliness and regularity. The child may express his aggression by soiling himself or by retaining his stool for long periods of time. In contrast, he may become so overly trained as to develop phobias about dirt, or a compulsive attitude that allows him to eliminate only at home and in an almost ritualistic manner.

> R. S., a three-and-a-half-year-old boy, was brought to the clinic because he was said to retain his stool for three or four days, and to have soiled his clothing regularly. The mother said the boy had been thoroughly toilet-trained by the time he was two years old. She had begun this training when he was a year old. Soon after the age of two he began the bowel retention and soiling. The symptoms were of great concern to the family and they discussed it with the child constantly. Enemas and laxatives of all kinds had been tried. X-rays of the boy's gastro-intestinal tract revealed a dilated colon; otherwise there was no somatic pathology, and the boy presented no behavior problems.
>
> The mother described herself as compulsively clean. Her first husband had left her because of her concern about cleanliness and he is reported to have said he is now married "to a real woman instead of an ice box." The present husband and the father of the boy is a policeman who expresses himself as liking his wife's cleanliness and orderliness. A daughter from the first marriage was also described as excessively neat.
>
> The mother said she tried to nurse her children, but it "never felt right," so she put them on feedings which were regularly scheduled. There was a younger sister toward whom the boy expressed much hostility and jealousy. He discussed his feeling that bowel movements are bad.
>
> The boy's parents were advised to ignore the boy's symptoms and to allow him more freedom and opportunity for rebellion. The child was treated by play therapy largely centered around finger painting, clay modeling, and other activities allowing dirtiness."

Toilet training is best begun when the child is capable of comprehending its meaning. This varies with individuals but ordinarily would be at age two or later. It should not be pushed at a time of stress as, for example, just after the birth of a younger sibling. A calm, tolerant attitude on the part of the mother is, of course, favorable. Shaming and scolding a child intensifies his anger and his anxiety. The use of enemas and suppositories should be avoided. This procedure robs the child of control of his own functions and is often reacted to with fear and rage.

Some parents do not see child's feeding and toilet training experiences as experiences by which he is gradually developing social attitudes and mastery of his environment, experiences through which his character is formed. Instead, these parents are largely concerned with using these interactions to impose their own attitudes on the child.

A person's character has been defined as his typical way of reacting. It is expressed in the capacity of the ego to balance primitive impulse with social-moral codes. Sigmund Freud has said that character represents an interchanging perpetuation of original impulses, a sublimation of these impulses, or reaction-formations against them.

By "interchanging perpetuation of original impulse" Freud indicated a persistence of motivation based on the wish for immediate gratification regardless of realistic and moral deterrants. It is essentially a refusal to adapt: a negative or avoidance response to externally imposed demands. We see it in two behavior patterns of the child — withdrawal and excessive rebellion. There may seem to be little similarity in these two patterns but both serve to perpetuate original impulse, one accomplishing this in fantasy and the other in acting-out behavior. The degree and the realistic suitability of rebellion determines its pathological potentiality. Some resistance to authority is, of course, healthy in children as in adults. It is only when a compulsive, repetitive pattern of resistance is established that the tendency becomes a handicapping personality trait. Such hostile, resistive people find it difficult to do anything that might be considered a duty, even through it be to their own advantage. They compulsively come late to work, put off or neglect assigned tasks, avoid studying for examinations, and the like, while protesting that they want to do these things but just "can't get at it." They drink excessively, or indulge in "forbidden" sexual behavior, not with any real enjoyment but on the basis of a need to defy moral precepts (even their own moral precepts). They are still battling with parent figures and their codes of behavior, and cannot flexibly give and take in a mature way.

The extreme example of the compulsively rebellious individual is the psychopathic (sociopathic) personality. This is the person who in his social behavior acts out his neurotic protests. We call the protests neurotic because they are the expression of turmoil within himself, rather than reactions to a realistic immediate situation. Such a person may steal, rape or kill for no apparent reason. He may never use the things he steals, may have had legitimate opportunities for sexual gratification, and may have no relationship with the stranger he kills. He acts compulsively and repetitively. After the act he may express recognition of the unacceptability of his behavior and may say he will not repeat it. However, in most cases such a statement means nothing, and sooner or later the person will repeat his antisocial acts. One must assume that though he is intellectually aware of codes of morality, he is not capable of using them to modify his violent, destructive impulses.

Sociopathic behavior of this kind is usually evident early in life. Some observers have suggested that it is indicative of an inborn defect, an incapacity for superego development. This has even been called "moral imbecility." The early development and the typical lack of responsiveness to treatment lend plausibility to this theory. However, knowing as we do the potent effect of early environment on character formation, we would hesitate to dismiss these social deviants as merely genetically handicapped people. Granting the variability of innate resources for social adaptation, we must grant also the modifiability of these resources by personal interaction. In many cases it would be difficult to assign blame to either heredity or environment alone as the following case illustrates.

C. has been in psychiatric treatment almost continuously

since early childhood. She is the only child of wealthy, socially prominent people. Her parents describe her as having been "always difficult." She slept poorly as a baby and as soon as she was able to walk she would run away at every opportunity. "You couldn't put her down and expect she'd stay there. She would take off. We were forever running after her." She quarreled with other children and often hit them. From kindergarten on, school was a problem. Various private and public schools were tried and in all of them she refused to do her work, often truanted, and always ended by being refused re-admittance. She was a beautiful girl with good average intelligence, but she never seemed able to use her resources constructively. In adolescence she began to drink excessively and became involved in various sexual relationships. At present, she is in a private psychiatric hospital where it is hoped that long-continued intensive psychotherapy can help her.

This young woman describes her early relationships with her parents as inconsistent and confusing. Her mother had not wanted children and had been married ten years before her birth. She reared her "by the book," apparently with little spontaneous warmth and understanding. The child was often left in the care of various maids. The father was proud of his pretty daughter, and liked to show her off, but was sharply critical of her if she did not perform satisfactorily. She states that she feared his violent temper but also feared his affectionate approaches which repelled her by their intensity and inconsistency. She never felt she could confide in her cold, detached mother. Her early rebellion against the parents was carried over to all authority figures and to the expectations which they had of her. The trust in parents and identification with them which form the basis for favorable superego development were lacking here. On the surface, the girl's situation seemed good, and neither of her parents could see that they had contributed in any way to her difficulties.

The child's battle with the demands of his social environment may be resolved not by overt rebellion but by a very different technique: that of over-adaptation or over-compensation. His hostility is concealed, often even from himself, by extreme conformity, perfectionism, prudery. Such a child becomes a compulsive person, exact and formal in his behavior, rigid in his interpretations of correctness. Compulsiveness, like all neurotic manifestations, varies in degree from a commonly occurring and not too disabling character trait to its exaggerated expression in compulsive-obsessive neurosis.

The compulsive child ordinarily is not recognized as having a problem though his parents may realize that he is tense and easily disturbed by changes in routine. Typically, he is obedient and exact about his responsibilities but often has outbursts of contrasting behavior, such as irritability and temper tantrums. He is lacking in warmth and spontaneity and seems to be motivated by the letter rather than the spirit of the law. His social concepts have been built on fear, rather than on love, hence he has not really accepted the social mores and must use rigid methods of self-control to avoid expressing his hostility and resistance.

If the child continues in these character traits into adult life he may sublimate them in socially acceptable ways. He may find work that places rewards on exactness and allows him a high degree of control. He will have difficulty in forming close personal relationships but he may discharge his formal responsibilities well. In such individuals there is great discrepancy between their own concept of themselves and their actual impulses and motivations. They tend to see themselves as righteous people with high standards of behavior, expecting perfection of themselves and of others, denying the hostile and distrustful attitudes which underlie their need for such rigid control.

It is when experiences occur which do not allow adequate sublimation, or which force recognition of the underlying conflicts, that the bizarre symptoms of compulsive-obsessive neurosis develop. In this disorder the patient's need for self-control becomes symbolized in ritualistic acts or repetitive thoughts. He realizes that his symptoms are unrealistic and unwarranted (which differentiates him from the psychotic patient) but he feels unable to control them.

A full-blown compulsive-obsessive syndrome is not common in childhood but it does occur.

L. A., a ten-year-old boy, was referred to the Psychiatry Clinic for what was described as "evening-up behavior." This meant that any time he touched something with one hand he would have to touch it with the other hand. If anything touched him on one foot he would then have to touch it with the other foot. If he brushed up against a building with his right hip he would then have to turn and brush up against it with his left hip. This behavior had been gradually increasing in intensity over the preceding year. Initially the parents had seen it only as a mannerism; however, it was becoming apparent to them that this was not normal behavior.

The patient had been the oldest of three children. A twin brother had died three years previously from an unusual metabolic disease. There was a sister three years younger. Father and mother were well-educated, cultured people. Father had always been very much wrapped up in his work as a University professor. He had always tended to bring work home with him. His graduate students had free access to the home, and his wife described the family as consisting of "my husband, myself, two children and three graduate students who are here every evening." The father and the students locked themselves in the study in the evening to go over their experimental results.

The mother presented these facts without appearing to be upset. In the initial interview she discussed the death of her younger son with calmness, coolness, and detachment. In a similar manner she presented a history of her own growing up. It appeared that she also had a strongly obsessive-compulsive character structure.

It was speculated that the child had developed an obsessive-compulsive syndrome as a way of controlling his aggressive impulses and feelings. Disturbing environmental situations were the father's neglect and the mother's cold, undemonstrative attitude. The brother's long illness and death, it was felt, might also have added to the child's anxiety. It was initially felt that an optimal therapeutic course should involve treatment of mother, father, and child. The parents initially wanted treatment only for the child and could not accept the need of therapy for themselves. However, a few weeks after the child was started in psychotherapy a family crisis developed during which the father expressed anger at his wife's coldness and hinted at developing interest in another woman. At this time both parents expressed willingness for consultation. The mother's treatment appeared to be the pivotal aspect of the care of this family. As she gradually worked through her need to separate feelings from thoughts she was able to become warmer with her family and to be capable also of permitting more aggression in her son. She and her husband faced more frankly the nature of their relationship with each other and, as a result, the husband withdrew some of his interest from his work and spent more time with his family. As the child slowly developed a trusting relationship with his therapist, he began very cautiously and afterward more openly to express his feelings.

After about a year of treatment he began talking about the period when his brother was sick, and gradually brought out his ambivalent feelings toward the brother and his guilty feelings after the brother's death. He had felt that his hostile feelings were responsible for the brother's death and, consequently, had become extremely fearful of his own aggressivity. A combination of treatment of parents and child led to good progress in the child.

A child such as this obviously presents his doctor with a psychiatric problem. Less obvious and often overlooked completely is the child with compulsive-obsessive character traits of less bizarre nature. These traits nevertheless may be establishing a foundation for more or less serious difficulties in later life. The child's need to be overly exact and controlled indicates that he is defending himself against his own internal conflicts and insecurities. The physician who is in good rapport with the patient and his family will recognize the need for understanding and helping to alleviate these tensions.

SUMMARY

Aggressive behavior in the child is an expression of his struggle for autonomy. He strives to express himself and, in so doing, must deal with the suppressing forces of his environment. In this struggle, he gradually develops a code of social behavior—his superego—which automatically controls, modifies and redirects his innate aggression. Over-intimidation, inconsistency, or lack of firmness on the part of parents create difficulties in superego formation. As a result, the child may develop symptoms ranging from overt over-aggressiveness to a state of anxious, compulsive conformity. In extreme cases, he may become the sociopathic adult or the seriously handicapped compulsively neurotic adult.

SUGGESTED READING

Allen, F. H.: Aggression in relation to emotional development, *Mental Hygiene, 34:*353, 1950.

Caplan, G.: *Emotional Problems of Early Childhood.* New York, Basic Books, Inc., 1955.

Eissler, K. (Ed.): *Searchlights on Delinquency.* New York, International Universities Press, 1949.

Freud, A.: Aggression in relation to emotional development. *Psychoanalytic Study of the Child, III-IV,* 1949.

Notes on aggression, *Bull. Menninger Clinic, 13:*143, 1949.

Gerard, Margaret: *The Emotionally Disturbed Child.* New York, The Child Welfare League of America, Inc.

Glueck, S. and Glueck, E. T.: *Unraveling Juvenile Delinquency.* New York, The Commonwealth Fund, 1950.

Hartman, H., Kris, E., and Lowenstein, R.: Notes on the theory of aggression. *Psychoanalytic Study of the Child, III-IV,* 1949.

Josselyn, I. M.: *The Happy Child,* New York, Random House, 1955.

Pearson, G. H. J.: *Emotional Disorders of Children.* New York, Norton, 1949.

Richmond, S., Eddy, E., and Garrad, S.: The syndrome of fecal soiling. *American Journal of Orthopsychiatry, 24:*391, 1954.

Chapter IV

Problems of Self-Identification

THE INFANT's basic need for nourishment, physical and psychic, and his need for self-expression motivate him to interact with the world around him. His needs cannot be satisfied in isolation. He must get and give, make demands and satisfy the demands of others, and in the process become a socialized human being. In these interactions he gradually develops the concept of his position as an individual. He judges people according to their behavior toward him and sees his environment as kind or cruel, tolerant or repressive, challenging or frightening, depending on his experiences with it.

Everyone's earliest ideas of himself in the world become the foundations for his personality. They are firmly established and though later experiences may contradict these ideas they still remain, consciously or unconsciously, to shape the life pattern. A sense of inferiority, for example, or a deep-rooted distrust, originating in the first years of life predispose to neurosis and to social maladjustments. These attitudes tend to create circular reactions; unsureness and withdrawal lead to failure which predisposes to further failure, and the child's image of himself as inferior and unwanted is fortified. Rejection leads to hostility which provokes further rejection and the child begins to see other people as his enemies. Negative self-concepts such as these may, if extreme, lead to serious mental disorder; in less extreme forms they still contribute to unfavorable personality traits.[1]

Bowlby, in his classical study of maternal care in relation to mental health[2] quotes observations by Goldfarb and others indicating the close correlation between maternal deprivation and developmental defects.

[1]Erikson, E. H.: *J. Am. Psychoanalytic Assn.*, IV: 1956.
[2]Bowlby, J.: *Maternal Care and Mental Health.* Geneva, World Health Organization, 1952.

TABLE VI

DIFFERENCES BETWEEN CHILDREN WHO HAD SPENT THEIR FIRST
THREE YEARS IN AN INSTITUTION AND CONTROLS WHO HAD NOT
(GOLDFARB)

Function Tested or Rated	Test or Rating Method	Result Expressed as	Results Institution Group	Control Group
Intelligence	Wechsler	mean IQ	72.4	95.4
Ability to conceptualize ...	Weigl .... Vigotsky	mean score ..... mean score	2.4 0.5	6.8 4.7
Reading	standard tests ...	mean score	5.1	6.8
Arithmetic	standard tests ...	mean score	4.7	6.7
Social maturity	Vineland Scale completed by case-workers	mean social quotient	79.0	98.8
Ability to keep rules .... Guilt on breaking rules	frustration ..... experiment	number of children ..... number of children	3 2	12 11
Capacity for relationships	case-worker's assessment ...	number of children able to make normal relationships ..	2	15
Speech		number of children up to average	3	14
Number of children (total)			15	15

Note: In the case of all differences shown, P is less than .01.

In these tables Goldfarb[1] has compared the mental and
emotional development of a group of fifteen children brought up
until the age of about three in an institution with fifteen children
reared in foster homes. In both groups, the children had been
given up by their mothers before nine months of age. The institution was hygenically satisfactory but allowed the infants
a bare minimum of personal attention. "They lived in almost
complete social isolation during their first year of life." Gold-

---

[1]Goldfarb, W.: *J. Exp. Educ.* 12:106, 1943.

TABLE VII

INCIDENCE OF PROBLEMS IN CHILDREN WHO HAD SPENT THEIR
FIRST THREE YEARS IN AN INSTITUTION AND CONTROLS WHO HAD
NOT (GOLDFARB)

			Results	
Problem	*Rated by*	*Result Expressed as*	*Institution Group*	*Control Group*
Unpopular with other children	case-worker	number of children showing problem	6	1
Craving affection	"	" "	9	2
Fearful	"	" "	8	1
Restless, hyperactive	"	" "	9	1
Inability to concentrate	"	" "	10	0
Poor school achievement	"	" "	15	1
Number of children (total)....			15	15

Note: In all cases but the first, P is less than .01. In the first case, it lies between .05 and .02.

farb's tables summarize some of the differences in development of the two groups of children.

We have already observed that newborn babies differ a great deal in the activity or passivity of their reactions. This variability seems to be apparent in fact even before birth. In the newborn it affects his feeding pattern and very early determines the attitudes of his parents toward him. The overly passive infant who makes few demands is often accepted as a good baby and thus rewarded for his passivity. This attitude intensifies his constitutional tendency, and as he develops he may find it easier to continue to be non-aggressive and relatively inactive. Such a child needs stimulation and encouragement to express himself, but unless he has understanding parents he is unlikely to get it; instead he is often allowed to develop a relatively introverted, withdrawn way of life. He allows himself little opportunity to try out his strength in interaction with other people. When frustrated or attacked, he tends to retreat rather than hold his ground.

His aggressive potentialities may come out in negative, resistive ways in the so-called passive aggression described in the previous chapter. He may become a feeding problem, may be enuretic or may be resistive and apprehensive about learning, particularly in new and unsupervised situations. In school the passive child is not considered to be a problem. His busy teacher is occupied by her overly active pupils. Here, as at home, he seldom gets the patient and persistent individual attention which would help him establish self confidence and experience in group relationships.

The passive child, lacking the satisfactions of participation and achievement, often develops into the withdrawn, dependent adult, handicapped by a sense of inferiority. He may find solace in reading, watching television, or in the company of a few others like himself who function on the periphery of the group. He may, however, use such talents as he has in creative activities which allow him to perform significantly while avoiding direct competition with his peers.

One of the most common symptoms presented by the adult who seeks psychiatric help is a sense of inadequacy. "I feel inferior, have no confidence, become shy and tense in a group."

Such attitudes begin in early childhood. If they are allowed to persist into adolescence, they usually become exaggerated at that time by the sharpened competitiveness within the group and the need to break away from the protective parent. An unsatisfactory social orientation restricts the opportunities for casual and relaxed relationships with young people of the opposite sex, and favors sexual anxieties and introversion.

A tendency to withdrawal perpetuates itself in a vicious circle of maladaptation. The child retreats from challenge and hence fails, and the sense of failure encourages further retreat. Fantasy becomes a tempting substitute for the discouragements of reality. We observe that the problems of the withdrawn child become intensified in adolescence when the need for independent activity and competition with peers are sharpened. What happens as he becomes an adult?

Although withdrawal is a very inefficient response it does not necessarily lead to serious psychopathology. Whether or not it does depends to a large extent on the social environment. In a not-too-demanding situation many withdrawn persons find a niche for themselves. Unless stimulated by the understanding interest of another person, they remain shy and inhibited, functioning on a minimum level of self support. If, however, in adolescence or early adult life they are fortunate enough to find sympathetic and perceptive friends and lovers, they may be encouraged to develop more confidence in their own resources and to struggle with the tendencies to retreat. The introvert does not become the extrovert but he may develop a socially constructive and self-sufficient way of life.

In many instances, the outcome is not so favorable. Frustrated in his attempts to realize adult goals, a shy and inhibited person may make neurotic compensations. He may become a hypochondriac, finding in illness an excuse for his failures. He may become alcoholic as the pressures of reality become increasingly intolerable and he must deaden his sensibility to them. Sometimes he finds solace in fantasies of significance, assuming, for example, that he is destined to be a great writer or artist or an intellectual and that some day his talents will be discovered. Such attitudes are common among the so-called "beat" groups in our culture. Within such groups there are, of course, some who do have artistic talent and are able to express themselves in creative productions even though their lives are socially restricted.

Adaptation by withdrawal becomes most pathologic when it progresses in the direction of schizophrenia. This is by no means an infrequent development. Schizophrenic patients make up a large proportion of first admissions to state hospitals and because of their chronicity they constitute the major share of the population of these hospitals. In addition, many thousands of schizoid, paranoid or overtly schizophrenic people are cared for at home or in private institutions or, in some cases, are able to make a marginal kind of social adjustment.

A fully developed schizophrenic psychosis is rare in childhood but the attitudes and experiences conducive to it may be evident in early life. We see them in the child who withdraws emotionally from warm interchange of close personal relationships, who seems suspicious and unresponsive and inclined to solitary activities. Such a child and his parents are seriously in need of psychiatric help.*

In contrast to the too-passive child, the overly active hyperkinetic child is restless, demanding and intolerant of frustration. Here, too, is seen exhibited a pattern of interaction with the parent. The childs behavior meets with disapproval, to which he reacts with increased demands.

A mother brought her two daughters, aged seven and five, to the clinic following a suicide attempt of the father, which had disturbed both children. The history indicated that the younger girl had always been a hyperactive problem child. She was described as restless, mischievous, with poor attention span. Her relationship with children was quarrelsome and dominating. The mother said she had never been able to control this child. She didn't apply herself well to her kindergarten activities.

In contrast, the older child had never been considered to be a problem, though the mother said she had sometimes noticed that the child was withdrawn and had little contact with other children. She did well in school and the teacher had never reported any concern about her. Following the father's suicide attempt, the older girl said she should die too, and seemed very depressed. The younger child expressed her disturbance more hysterically. Psychological tests indicated more serious pathology in the older child with marked inability to relate to other people. The younger girl's test indicated impulsiveness and poor control, but better contact. There was much tension in this family, and the older girl had reacted to it by withdrawal, the younger by rebellion. Treatment was directed toward the external problems of the parents. They were encouraged toward a more firm attitude with the younger child, and toward a more understanding and encouraging attitude toward the older girl.

The too-active child needs parents who love him consistently but insist on reasonable control. Unfortunately, his behavior exhausts and antagonizes his parents, who may react in either extreme of helpless indulgence or rigid restraint. A battle for dominance is set up and whatever the result, no one wins. If the parents weakly capitulate, and out of guilt or anxiety allow

*Bender, L.: Childhood Schizophrenia. *Psychiatric Quart.*, 27:663, 1953.

the child restlessly to follow his impulses, the child lacks a sense of parental strength and understanding. He senses the rejection underlying the pampering. He continues to make demands and to seek immediate gratification which never satisfies.

If, on the other hand, the parents of the hyperkinetic child go to the opposite extreme of rigid, formalistic restraint, the child's aggression becomes pent up to an intolerable degree and is expressed destructively at every opportunity.

As the too-passive child tends to become the withdrawn adult, so the too-active child can become the impulse-driven adult. He may develop into the never-do-well, flitting from one role to another, never consistently working toward a goal. His intolerance of frustration may lead him into alcoholism or delinquency. His insatiable quest for immediate achievement represents his attempt at denial of his basic goallessness and dissatisfaction in himself.

Excessive passivity and excessive impulsive activity both represent an inability or unwillingness to deal directly and realistically with the problem of adaptation. By withdrawal, one avoids the necessity to struggle, to assume initiative and to formulate goals. The challenging impacts of the milieu are avoided and one settles for a constricted world in which gratifying fantasies may act as substitutes for the more tangible rewards of achievement. The withdrawn person is usually found to have a conflictual and ambivalent concept of himself. He is shy and unresponsive with people and realizes his inadequacy in social situations. At the same time, he has developed fantasies of self-glorification which allow him to believe he is superior. Fantasy and reality vacillate, and the result is confusion in self-identification. In those unfortunate cases where the distinctions break down and the dream becomes a reality, the result is psychosis.

The impulsive, over-active person is avoiding adaptation in a quite different but also ineffective way. He seeks avidly for immediate satisfaction. He may ignore denials and restraint, demanding his way regardless of social code, or he may turn away from a frustrating situation, going aimlessly from one experience to another.

The poorly adaptive nature of behavior patterns such as these makes the need for early prophylaxis evident. Allowing for the natural inclinations of the child, it is still possible for him to modify these inclinations in the direction of good social integration.

Parents are models for their children. The boy or girl who loves and admires his parents wants to be like them. He imitates them and assumes their attitudes. In an active way, too, the parents who understand and appreciate their children's needs, their abilities and handicaps, can help them form a consistent and realistic self-identification. There are, however, many family and community situations which interfere with a good parent-child rapport.[1]

When the parents are maladjusted, they express their discontent in various ways on their children. For example, the wife who is antagonistic to her husband may reject the child who resembles him or his family in appearance and mannerisms.

A mother introduced her family by saying, "I have two boys and a bad little girl." She described the daughter as looking and acting like her father. "The boys resemble my family." The parents were separated. This active little girl responded to her mother's idea of her by disobedience and attention-getting behavior and was becoming known as a problem child.

Another mother, a beautiful, pampered woman, was so disappointed by the fact that her daughter inherited the coarser and heavier appearance of the father's family, that she was never able to establish a warm, understanding relationship with her. The child was obviously unhappy. Unable to compete with her mother, and feeling rejected by her, she thwarted every attempt of the parent to shape her into her own image. She cultivated sloppiness, was resistive and seclusive and though highly intelligent, refused to perform in school except in her work with one understanding teacher who sensed the meaning of her defenses.

A sense of inadequacy in comparison with other family members may develop even when the parents try not to discriminate. A boy who is small and frail may find comparison with a strong, vigorous brother very handicapping. He may over-compensate

---

[1]Spitz, R. A.: *Mental Health Today*, Vol. VII.

for his size by tough behavior or may, on the other hand, become withdrawn and unsure of himself.

Fathers often prefer one daughter over another, giving the rejected child a conviction of her own unacceptability as a female. This can lead to serious consequences as we will see when we study the problems of sexual identification.

A child of average intelligence may consider himself stupid in a family of high scholastic achievement. In a less ambitious, less intelligent family such a child would develop a very different image of himself. Unhappy situations of this kind often can develop when a cultured couple adopt a child who is incapable of educational progress compared to the family's standards.

> C. T., an adopted boy of ten, was referred for psychiatric help because he was doing poorly in school. His parents were highly educated people of superior intelligence. The boy's I.Q. was average. The father had planned that the boy would go to college and had always tried to interest him in his own scientific field. The boy tried hard in school at first, but recently had apparently given up and was performing below his intellectual capacity. He expressed feelings of inferiority, had been truanting from school and otherwise rebelling against authority.
>
> The father showed little capacity for warmth. The mother seemed to have affection for the boy but shared the father's disappointment in him. Both parents were cooperative with the psychiatric consultants, and the mother especially was able to make fundamental changes in attitude in her approach to the boy with resulting improvement in his adjustment.

The rejected child is handicapped, but so is the one who is the object of too-intense parental attachment. A mother whose needs for love are frustrated by the mate sometimes turns to the children for fulfillment of these needs. This may apply equally to the father. The children may accept this and flourish under it during the first years of life, but as they try to achieve independence they find it hard to break away, and when they do succeed in doing so, they are torn by feelings of guilt and disloyalty. Many a bachelor "mama's boy" and spinster "daddy's girl" are unable to reach a mature psychosexual development because of these attachments.

N. M., a fourteen-year-old girl, was reported to have recently become alienated from her friends and her social activities and to spend a good deal of time alone. She did not confide in either of her parents, but they could observe that she was very unhappy. This family had three daughters, aged seventeen, fourteen, and nine. The first child had always been close to her mother. Following the birth of N., the second girl, the mother became depressed and withdrawn for several months. Apparently to compensate for this, the father lavished a great deal of attention on this girl, and he continued to do so with relative disregard of the older child. The youngest daughter, aged nine, seems to have been accepted more casually by both parents. When N. entered pubescence, the father's attitude toward her changed. He became cold, more restrained and was less permissive with her than he was with the older sister. He seemed especially disturbed by N.'s interest in boys and group activities. Her symptoms appeared in apparent response to those changes in his relationship with her. The older girl, who had been allowed more freedom, had a confiding relationship with her mother and appeared to be relatively well-adjusted. N. expressed a good deal of angry and confused feelings about her relationship with her parents. She said she felt neither of them liked her. Though she had previously had boy and girl friends, she now avoided boys and felt ill at ease with girls when they talked about them.

It was obvious that this child's adolescent development had been interfered with by an originally too-close attachment to the father, followed by his withdrawal as he began to see her as a young woman. The older girl, despite the father's relative disinterest, had found a satisfactory feminine identification in her good relationship with the mother. The mother's jealousy of N.'s attachment to the father and the girl's own possessive strivings for his affections had prevented her from establishing a good rapport with her mother. She had never satisfactorily resolved her feeling about her parents and was, consequently, handicapped in achieving psychosexual maturity.

Similar, though expressed very differently symptomatically, were the problems of a boy of fifteen who had been very closely related to his mother since the death of his father when the boy was ten. The mother encouraged this closeness by sleeping in the same bedroom with him for a year after the father's death, taking him with her wherever she went and talking with him about all his activities. He seemed to accept this situation, and had no overt difficulties until early adolescence when he became rebellious and defiant toward his mother. During his first psychiatric consultation he talked of obsessive thoughts of killing his mother. The thoughts terrified him, but he could not control them. He often dreamed of being closed in or smothered. These anxieties were severely interfering with his school and social adjustments, and it was felt that a long period of therapy would be necessary, and that the mother also would have to be treated.

We have already referred to the damaging effects of lack of adequate mothering. Bowlby[1] emphasizes the fact that serious emotional and intellectual retardation, as well as physical maldevelopment, result from extreme deprivation. An inconsistent, ambivalent or shifting attitude on the part of the parent is likewise reflected in personality defects. Whereas the totally rejected child tends to withdraw and lose capacity for close personal relationships, the inconsistently treated child often develops a defensive, antisocial response.

Some interesting studies have been made of the specific effect of the mother-child relationship at different ages in boys and girls. Boys appeared to be more sensitive to maternal hostility in infancy but reacted violently against maternal over-protection in adolescence. Girls, on the other hand, were not as obviously affected by rejection in early childhood, but reacted badly to it in adolescence and were more accepting of over-protection than were the adolescent boys.

As the child becomes aware of himself as a group member, it becomes important for him to be like the other members of the group. The "different" child is discriminated against and develops a sense of unhappy alienation. These differences may be obvious or may be subtle and apparently trivial. Even so small a thing as a slight deviation in dress — a skirt too long or a jacket out of style — may set a child apart in his group and create a sense of unsureness and unacceptability in him. A little

[1]Bowlby, J.: *Maternal Care and Mental Health*. W. H. O. Report, 1951, p. 22.

boy gets off to a bad start in forming a self impression if his mother waits too long to have his curls cut off. Divergencies in physical maturation often create problems. The boy who is small for his age, the overly tall girl, the child whose sexual maturation is either too early or too late, are somewhat handicapped in their group adjustment.

L. V., a sixteen-year-old girl, came in for help because of depression. She had recently been crying a great deal and withdrawing from her friends. She had been apparently well adjusted until about a year before. The girl's family belonged to a very strict religious group which disapproved of make-up, dating, dancing, and attractive dressing. The girl attended high school in a sophisticated community. She had been a good student but recently seemed to lose interest.

Interviews with the parents indicated that as the girl reached adolescence the mother became increasingly repressive with her, especially warning her about having anything to do with boys. The mother herself had a good deal of anxiety about sex, which she had rationalized by religious restrictions. When the girl became depressed the parents advised her to pray. Her pastor, however, recognized the child's disturbance as related to her sense of difference in the group, and he advised psychiatric referral.

The degree of seriousness of deviations from the norm depends on the resources of the child for dealing actively with his situation. If he is confident and aggressive, he may force recognition and respect from the group even though he departs in some detail from the normal. If, however, he is sensitive and unsure of himself, he may be tortured by being teased and may retreat into a defensive pattern that forms an unfavorable foundation for his personality development.

M. S., a girl of fifteen, was referred by the school counselor because of an unhappy attitude and a tendency to avoid group activities. The child seemed sullen and unresponsive at first, but soon began to express a sense of inferiority and difference related to her inability to afford the clothes and the activities of her peers. The family lived in a wealthy community. The parents were well educated but the father, a school teacher, earned a moderate salary. The mother was socially ambitious and the girl had taken over these ambitions, but was unable to realize them. She felt pushed by the mother, angry at the mother's expectations of her and at her own inability to satisfy them.

In contrast to this girl was one in similar circumstances in the same community, but belonging to a family of high cultural standards and low social-climbing aspirations. This girl, though more poorly dressed than the other children and lacking such assets as a car and a country club membership, nevertheless won acceptance on the basis of her own friendly, confident manner and her talents. The difference lay in the more relaxed attitude of these parents toward themselves and their children, which favored, in the children, the development of a sense of values to sustain them in spite of some material deprivation.

The physical deviation of obesity creates difficulty in social adaptation. It is complicated by the fact that the obesity is both cause and effect of the problem. The fat child's obsessive need to eat replaces other forms of satisfaction. The mother sometimes encourages this by giving the child food instead of love: feeding him liberally and well, feeling that in this way she is being a good mother.

One woman who suffered much from obesity in her youth said, "Mother never listened and never tried to understand what was going on with me, but if I was unhappy she would poke food at me and prepare special diets for me. She pooh-poohed my protests that my fatness was part of my difficulty."

Another patient, who had been called "Fatso" as a boy, described his father as "rejecting, critical, never satisfied with me," and his mother as "cold and remote, almost martyrish in looking after our needs. She was an excellent cook and encouraged me to eat, but I never had any demonstration of love from either of them."

M. N., a girl aged eight, was brought in because of overweight and because she appeared to be unhappy, cried in school, and was rejected by the other children who called her "Fatty." She was the younger of two sisters. The ten-year-old sister also was overweight but did better in school and did have a few friends. The mother also was overweight.

Mother was a college graduate and bright; the father was a suspicious, withdrawn, intelligent man who was unable to give much to his family. Mother's history indicated that she had taken off weight while in college but after her marriage put on forty pounds and had never lost it. The mother had a tendency to eat excessively and to shove food at the children, especially when they seemed unhappy. Candy was in the home at all times, and mother and daughter seemed to take special pleasure in a good meal or in eating out in a restaurant. The mother had withdrawn progressively from interest in her husband, and he had, in recent years, shown some interest in other women. Shortly before the girl was brought in he had left the mother, and divorce proceedings were going on. The children seemed to feel torn between their parents.

Psychotherapy with this child was attempted with some results, as far as her depression was concerned, and with a little better social adjustment. The obesity problem, however, required that she cooperate in a program of self-control which she was unwilling to do. She was more interested in being taken care of by the therapist than in exerting herself to try to control the problem of the weight.

The mother of the obese child does not always urge him to eat. Sometimes she — and the entire family — make fun of him for doing so, but he eats in spite of them, even in a spirit of rebellion. He will often verbalize that he eats because he likes to. "It is the only fun I have."

Food greediness is one expression of the hunger to receive. One obese girl said, "I used to wake up every morning and look to see if anyone had brought me a gift in the night. Christmases and birthdays were looked forward to eagerly, but I never seemed to be satisfied with what I got; it never seemed to make me happy." This child's parents did give to her generously of material things, but she said she always felt "They wanted me to be different from the way I was. They were always trying to make me over."

Although the obese child is socially handicapped, he is seldom willing to give up the satisfactions directly and indirectly related to his state. He enjoys the food and he seems to enjoy his relatively withdrawn situation.

Hilda Bruch[1] describes the fat children she has studied as being, for the most part, passive and dependent on their mothers. They often use their dependency as a way of controlling their environment, being very demanding that the mother wait on them and give to them. Many of these mothers took a possessively protective, infantilizing attitude toward the children, thus encouraging the dependency and overeating. In other cases the parents' protective behavior seemed quite obviously to be an over-compensation for a rejection of the child.

If we think of obesity as a kind of adaptation, it becomes obvious that it cannot be satisfactorily treated merely by diet. A stringent restriction of food will usually be reacted to by resistance and cheating. If the child is forced to conform unwillingly, he may develop such serious reactions as depression, withdrawal, or extreme irritability. A more indirect, therapeutic approach is indicated. The parents' attitudes may have to be modified, if any success is to be achieved. It is sometimes possible to draw the passive fat child into more active group participation and to stimulate him to interests that can substitute for appetite gratification. This often happens spontaneously with the development of adolescence when appearance becomes increasingly important in determining group acceptance. If at adolescence the child cannot emancipate himself from his passive dependence on his parents, and continues obese, he remains depreciated by himself and others, because in our culture (unlike some other cultures) slimness is admired and the fat person is regarded with some degree of facetiousness and rejection.

Physical handicaps of any kind can interfere with good personality development. Poor vision necessitating the wearing of glasses is a common enough phenomenon to be very casually accepted by the group; it may, however, by interfering with a boy's active participation in sports, or by giving a girl the feeling that glasses make her less attractive, have some effect on the child's concept of himself.

A twelve-year-old boy was referred to psychiatry from the Ophthalmology Department. He had a visual defect partially

---

[1]Bruch, Hilda: *The Importance of Overweight*, New York, Norton, 1957.

corrected by glasses but the physicians had observed that he had not used his vision up to capacity. He was adjusting poorly at school and at home.

The boy said he had no friends and no interest in group activities. His factual information was poor.

The father was a tense person, absorbed in his work, who left the care of the children to his wife. The mother had a deprived background and had been sent to this country alone, when she was thirteen, to live with an aunt. She harbored resentment about the early years of neglect. Following marriage she was willing to work and put her husband through college. She had been reluctant, however, to have children but yielded to pressure from the husband, and became pregnant with the patient. Following his birth she became a devoted, over-protective mother. She said that at the time she learned of his visual handicap, when he was eighteen months old, she became depressed and had been depressed ever since.

Two years before the boy's referral, a brother had been born. The brother is described as normal in every way. The parents admitted that they enjoyed this child and had shifted much of their interest to him. C. began to show more overt disturbance following his brother's birth. Because of his visual handicap and his mother's previous over-protectiveness, he had become more than normally dependent on his parents and lacking in good peer relationships. As the parents shifted their relationship to the brother, he became withdrawn and spent a good deal of time apparently day-dreaming.

Therapy here was directed toward giving the parents a better understanding of the boy's feelings. They cooperated well and with a change in their attitudes the boy began to do better in school. His reading and his social confidence both improved though there was, of course, no objective change in his vision.

This situation indicates that the degree to which physical handicap interferes with good adaptation depends to a large extent on the attitudes of those people close to the child.

More serious physical defects, which set a child apart as noticeably different, create serious adaptive problems. Blindness and/or deafness necessitate a modified kind of life situation. The equanimity of the blind, however, has often been remarked upon and has been contrasted with the irritability and suspiciousness of the deaf. There seems to exist a human tendency to feel pity for the person whose vision is affected and to have a more rejecting attitude toward the one whose hearing is impaired. The latter defect is not so obvious, hence not so pitiful, and it is sometimes assumed that the deaf person is merely inattentive. His requests for repetition are found annoying and his misinterpretations facetious. These prevalent attitudes may explain the different personality reactions in the two handicapped groups. The life of Helen Keller is a clear illustration of the fact that a seriously handicapped person, if otherwise rich in personality resources and if treated with understanding and consideration, may identify himself as an acceptable and creative social individual.

Orthopedic crippling, as for example, congenital defects or paralyses following polio, brings up the question of whether a child so afflicted should attend regular or special school. If his family protects but doesn't discourage him, treats him much as it treats his siblings, and if he remains in a familiar group which accepts his handicap casually, he has probably the best situation for a normal personality development. Here, too, the success depends largely on the individual's capacity to compensate for his limitations by the use of interests and activities open to him.

It is evident that some handicapped children must be educated separately from their peers because of the severe nature of their disability. Children with sensory defects such as blindness or deafness should have the benefit of special instruction from specially trained teachers. Children with severe orthopedic disabilities, children with a significant degree of cerebral palsy and those with severe cardiac disease show significantly better progress if special arrangements are made for their education in separate classes. Similarly mentally retarded children need special supervision by teachers trained for their special type of instruction. Some effort should be made to integrate part of the activities of these children in school with those of children who are not physically nor educationally handicapped. Outside of school, maximal participation in activities with normal children, consistent with the safety of these handicapped children, should also be encouraged. Although it is true that education in special classes for these children will reinforce the concept that these children have of themselves as being different from the normal, this is consistent with the realities of their handicapping condition.

In contrast children with mild or moderate cardiac defects, children with innocent murmurs, children with mild orthopedic conditions and children with understature should in almost all instances attend regular school classes. There should be a minimum of restrictions associated with their special needs. Placing a child with a mild cardiac condition, for example, in a special school or a special class may lead to the development of self imposed restrictions by the child far in excess of his actual physical limitations. This may encourage the child to develop a distorted concept of himself as a severely handicapped individual and thus interfere with his further personality development and with his subsequent adjustment at home and in the community.

Parents of handicapped children may react unwisely in either of two directions. They may over-protect, pity and pamper the child, encouraging him to remain in the infantile, dependent state. Unless he is energetic and aggressive enough to rebel, he may, in this case, never achieve a responsible, mature development. This attitude is also unacceptable to the other children in the family, who tend to resent the parents' preoccupation with the weak one and to feel deprived of their share of parental affection.

An opposite attitude is that of parents who are ashamed of the defective child, are cold and rejecting to him and make no effort to help him deal with his serious problems of social adaptation. A sad illustration of this attitude was that of an eight-year-old boy with cleft palate brought by the mother to a clinic because of temper outbursts. The mother admitted that she was ashamed of the child and kept him in his room whenever anyone came to the house. She complained bitterly of being afflicted with such a son but had made no attempt to have any reparative surgery done or to make the child's life easier for him in any way. The boy was completely defeated, bitterly angry yet still able to respond to the unexpected kindness and understanding of the therapist. Plastic surgery, followed by supportive psychotherapy and work with the parents, effected a remakable transformation in this child's attitude toward himself and the world.

We see that the development of a satisfactory sense of identity depends largely on one's endowment in interaction with his family milieu. It is also affected by the cultural milieu acting either directly on the developing child or indirectly through his family. Poverty, for example, can have an inhibiting effect. It interferes not only with the child's respect for himself, but for his family as well. Living arrangements over-crowded and shabby allow for little personal dignity and are conducive to irritable or apathetic family relationships. If the child lacks admiration for his parents, he also, in identifying with them, lacks self-respect. Crowded conditions contribute also to sexual overstimulation, particularly if the children must sleep in the same room with the parents and are allowed to hear or see them in sexual intercourse. Such scenes may contribute to excessive sex play and sexual preoccupation on the part of the children.

A deprived economic situation seems to be most traumatic when it departs from the community norm. The children in a poor family then feel inferior to their peers and particularly resent the deprivation of material things enjoyed by the other children. Shabby, unsuitable clothing constitutes a handicap to the sense of belonging to the group.

Studies have indicated that low family income tends to correlate with emotional maladjustment, as well as with disabling physical illness. Inadequate diets and lack of cleanliness, by predisposing to frequent illness, may contribute to a sense of inadequacy.[1]

Although poverty on the whole has a negative effect on the personality development, it does not follow that satisfactory self-identification is quantitatively correlated with wealth. The children of extremely wealthy families can, in fact, be handicapped by the lack of challenge in their life situation, the easy gratifications, and often the lack of close contact with the mother. Too great an emphasis on material possessions and on social status can warp the standards of judgment by which the child evaluates himself and other people.

Children growing up in a culture reflect its traditions and the

---

[1]U.S. Public Health Service National Health Survey, 1945.

self-image is formulated with these traditions in the background. In our Western society there is a good deal of inconsistency between the prevalent Judeo-Christian admonishment to meekness and, in contrast, the obvious rewards which are given to aggressive and even ruthless competitiveness. This ambivalent attitude does not provide a solid foundation for moral standards. Young people too often see their adults giving lip service to religion while being motivated by the principle of "getting by." They hear tolerance and charity preached from the pulpit but see around them the existence of racial and religious intolerance and bigotry.

The effects of prejudice and social-religious discrimination are detrimental to those exposed to it. Prejudiced parents encourage their childen in narrow, self-righteous and hostile attitudes toward other people—attitudes which encourage aggression and cruelty. The victims of these intolerances also are warped in their personality development. A sense of alienation imposed on them may cause them to react by withdrawal, or by over-compensatory aggressiveness. The degree of trauma depends, of course, on the intensity of prejudice in the community. It depends, also, on the courage and solidarity of the family life. If a child is encouraged to respect and admire his inherited traditions, he need not lose faith in himself even though his peers treat him with unjust discrimination. It is unfortunate when children of minority groups take over a disrespect for their own group and try to identify with the more fortunately situated majority. Unable satisfactorily to accomplish this, and having rejected their own group identification, they are inclined to join a "gang" of some kind to establish a place for themselves. The high rate of delinquency among the Negro and Puerto Rican adolescents in the United States seems to be related to the fact that these young people have taken over the depreciating attitudes of the white-American community toward themselves and their families, hence they have no solid sense of self in group identification and no traditionally established goals and mores.

A satisfactory sense of identification begins with the feeling about one's own resources. The child who is constitutionally intelligent enough and physically competent enough to hold his own in his environment has a favorable beginning. There are also, undoubtedly, other innate resources which are more difficult to define and to separate from the effects of early environmental impact. Such qualities as emotional stability, capacity for flexible adaptation, imaginativeness and creative potential are illustrative of such innate resources. These qualities are not as fixed by heredity as one's I.Q. or the color of one's eyes, but they are surely, to some degree, inborn. The child well endowed in resources has a more varied repertoire of reactive possibilities to deal with stress and strain, hence he is strongly determined toward a satisfactory concept of himself.

The feeling for one's own capacity soon merges with feelings about one's family. The boy and girl who admire their father and mother borrow strength from these relationships. They see themselves not only in terms of their own resources but those of their parents as well. The little child's loyalty to the family tends to be quite unquestioning, but as the child grows older he judges his parents more objectively. If he is disillusioned in his early trust and respect, he loses not only confidence in them but in himself. The family attitudes and aptitudes that he has incorporated no longer seem solid; in depreciating them, he depreciates himself.[1]

We have discussed the importance of group acceptance of the individual. The individual's acceptance of the group is also important. One's identification within the group can be a source of strength or of weakness. The individual likes to be proud of his community and his country. A dilapidated neighborhood breeds delinquency; likewise, national corruption can bring out the worst potentialities in its citizens. Blind obedience to a dictatorial regime stifles originality, favors intolerance and monotony of thinking. The individual is lost in the mass.

SUMMARY

The young child's impressions of himself in relation to the world, formed in the first years of life, become the foundation for his adult personality. They are determined by interaction

---

[1]Erikson, E. H.: *Problems of Infancy and Childhood.* J. Macy, Jr. Foundation, 1950.

between the child, with his constitutionally-determined resources, and the impact of his social environment. Endogenous factors which set the child apart make social integration difficult. Family attitudes toward him are of greatest importance and these attitudes reflect to some degree those of the culture. The recognition and treatment of unfavorable early self-concepts of the child may constitute effective prophylactic psychiatry.

SUGGESTED READINGS

Bowlby, J.: *Maternal Care and Mental Health.* Geneva W. H. O. Monograph Series No. 2, 1952.

Bowlby, J.: Grief and Mourning in Infancy and Early Childhood. *Psychoanalytic study of the Child, XV:9,* 1960.

Bruch, H.: *The Importance of Overweight.* New York, W. W. Norton, 1957.

Buxbaum, E.: A contribution to the psychoanalytic knowledge of the latency period, *Am. J. Orthopsych., 21:*182, 1951.

Caplan, G. (Ed.): *Prevention of Mental Disorders in Children.* New York, Basic Books, 1961.

Children's Bureau: *Emotional Problems Associated with Handicapping Conditions in Children.* Washington Fed. Security Agency, 1952.

Clarke, A. B., and Clarke, A. M.: Some recent advances in the study of early deprivation. *Child Psychology and Psychiatry, 1:*26, 1960.

Bender, L., and Freedman, A. M.: A study of the first three years in the maturation of schizophrenic children, *Quarterly J. of Child Behavior, IV:*245, 1952.

Erickson, E. H.: *Childhood and Society.* New York, Norton, 1950.

Escalona, S. K.: Patterns of infantile experience and the developmental process. *Psychoanalytic Study of the Child, XVIII:*197, 1963.

Freud, Anna: *The Ego and the Mechanism of Defense.* London, Hogarth Press, 1948.

Freud, Anna: The concept of developmental lines. *Psychoanalytic Study of the Child, XVIII:*245, 1963.

Henry, J., and Warson, S.: Family structure and psychic development, *Am. J. Orthopsych., 21:*59, 1951.

Jackson, D. D.: The question of family homeostatis, *Psych. Quart.* Supplement *31:*79, 1957.

Kanner, L.: Problems of nosology and psychodynamics in early infantile autism, *Am. J. of Orthopsych., XIX:*416, 1949.

Lampl-De Groot, J.: Ego Ideal and Superego. *Psychoanalytic Study of the Child, XVII,* 1962.

Lippman, H. S.: *Treatment of the Child in Emotional Conflict.* New York, Blakeston, 1956.

Mahler, M. S.: On child psychosis and schizophrenia: autistic and symbiotic infantile psychoses, *Psychoanalytic Study of Child, VII,* 1952.

Murphy, L. B.: Childhood Experiences in Relation to Personality Development in *Personality and the Behavior Disorders, Hunt, J. McV. (Ed.):* New York, Ronald Press, 1944.

Rank, B.: Adaptation of the psychoanalytic technique for the treatment of children with atypical development, *Am. J. Orthopsych., XIX,* 1949.

Rank, B., and MacNaughton, D.: A clinical contribution to early ego development, *Psychoanalytic Study of Child, V,* 1950.

Redl, F.: The concept of ego disturbance and ego support, *Am. J. Orthopsych., 22:*273, 1952.

Piers, G. and Singer, M. B.: *Shame and Guilt.* Springfield, Chas. C Thomas, 1953.

Spitz, R. A.: Anaclitic depression, *The Psychoanalytic Study of Child,* 2:313, 1946.

Sullivan, H. S.: *The Interpersonal Theory of Psychiatry.* New York, W. W. Norton Co., 1953.

Chapter V

Problems of Sexual Identification

BEHAVIOR BASED on sexual difference is found in all higher animal forms. It has recently been demonstrated that much of this behavior, previously believed to represent the unfolding of genetically predetermined patterns, such as those found in invertebrate forms, is dependent on complex interrelationships normally present in the environment of the young animal. The development of the usual forms of behavior according to sexual identification appears dependent on imprinting[1] which must occur at the proper developmental period.

The problem is more complex in the human individual but much can still be learned from an examination of the biological factors underlying sexuality. It is apparent that what is considered as sexuality involves numerous complex biological and psychological factors. From a biological standpoint, the most fundamental difference between the sexes is found in the sex chromosomes. The normal female possesses two X chromosomes in each cell; the normal male, one X and one Y chromosome. Cytogenetic studies have revealed numerous other combinations of sex chromosomes in human individuals, such as XO, XXY, XXX, XXYY, and XXXY. In addition, there are many human individuals who are mosaic in cell constitution with more than one cell line present with differing sex chromosome pattern. Examples of mosaicism involving the sex chromosomes are XO/XX, XO/XXX, XO/XX/XXX and XX/XXY.

The Lyon[2] hypothesis, at present under study, proposes that only one X chromosome is biologically active in each cell with more than one X chromosome. The role of the Y chromosome

---

[1] Hess, E. H.: Imprinting, an effect of early experiences. *Science, 130:*133, 1959.

[2] McKusick, V. A.: *On the X-Chromosome of Man.* American Institute of Biological Science, Washington, D.C., 1964, pp. 60-68.

appears to be concerned with the differentiation of the indifferent gonads into testes. The role of the second X chromosome in the female is concerned primarily with the development of the normal ovary. The evidence fails to indicate that sex chromosomes in man have any other more direct influence on behavior.

The gonad, normally directed in its differentiation by the sex chromosomes present, plays a critical role in sexual development. In embryogenesis the experiments of Jost[3] have shown that the fetal testis is responsible for male differentiation from the primitive bisexual state. In the absence of testes the development of the internal and external genitalia proceeds along female lines. It is evident that in some instances fetal testicular influence may be faulty and incomplete, and that only partial male differentiation may occur. This is one of the most common causes for the development of hermaphroditism. Such individuals may be mistaken for normal females at birth. Gender role is firmly established before the effects of the endocrine secretion of the gonads at puberty are manifest. These hormones complete the sexual differentiation which is ordinarily in accord with the previously developed gender role.

Abnormalities in estrogenic and androgenic secretion are not infrequently encountered. In the case of virilizing adrenocortical hyperplasia, an inborn error of metabolism in the adrenal results in virilization of the female fetus. The external genitalia resemble those of the male although the internal genitalia remain female. Unless treated, virilization continues after birth in this condition. Similarly, some individuals with testes, only minimally differentiated along male lines, may develop breasts and a female body configuration at puberty. There are also individuals of varying chromosome configuration with both ovarian and testicular tissue. These individuals may be partially differentiated along male lines and may feminize or virilize at puberty or show evidence of both processes.

A study of the psychosexual development of patients with intersexuality has been of great interest and value in the study

---

[3]Jost, A.: The role of fetal hormones in pre-natal development. *The Harvey Lectures* 1959-60, Series 55, New York and London, Academic Press, 1961.

of the factors leading to normal sexual identification and behavior. It is clear that it is neither the sex chromosomes, the nature of the internal or external genitalia nor the secondary sex characteristics which determine sexual identification or gender role. These factors do play a permissive role. It has, however, been conclusively shown in hermaphroditism that it is the sex of assignment followed by the resulting appropriate treatment of the child as a boy or a girl within the family milieu which is critical.

One should not underestimate the problems faced by the individual with hermaphroditism. The normal individual is favored by the fact that as gender role develops in the second and third year of life and is reinforced in childhood, it is found by the individual to be consistent with the morphology of the internal and external genitalia and later with the proper development of secondary sex characteristics and the capacity for normal sexual intercourse and reproduction. In view of the fact that essentially normal gender role and sexual behavior consistent with sex assignment ordinarily develops in hermaphroditic individuals if the psychosocial factors within the family are favorable, it is not surprising that individuals who are normal biological males or females may develop various kinds of abnormal sexual identification and behavior as a result of unfavorable factors in the family setting which are operative as gender role emerges and is reinforced.

As the child develops a sense of personal identity he becomes aware of himself as masculine or feminine. This implies not only an awareness of anatomic distinction but also an awareness of the role he is expected to play as a boy or a girl. The role differs in detail in different cultures, but in Western cultures it correlates masculinity with strength, activity and dominance, femininity with receptivity, nurturance and decorativeness. Cultural traditions impose themselves on the child from the earliest years of life. The little girl is dressed up and praised for her prettiness; the little boy is encouraged to be tough. She is given dolls and toy dishes; he receives guns and sports equipment.

While the child is thus concerning himself with the masculine or feminine image, he is, at the same time, experiencing sexual sensations and curiosities. At first the feelings are diffuse and self-centered, later they become localized to the genitals and responsive to other people.

There are therefore two distinct, though at times overlapping, developmental paths. First the child must integrate his sexual feelings in an individually and socially acceptable way. Second, he must — again to his own satisfaction and that of his social milieu — feel identified as a boy or as a girl.

Difficulties in the areas of sexuality per se are frequently observed in children. They are, in most cases, quite clearly the result of exposure to distorted attitudes of other people, particularly the parents. The problems are presented to the pediatrician by way of complaints of excessive masturbation, sex play or sexual curiosity. The opposite form of behavior — that of excessive inhibition of sexual interest — is seldom presented as a problem by the parents though it, too, may be indicative of disturbed, conflicting feelings.

The infant's first pleasurable sensations are oral and diffusely tactile. Sucking relieves his tensions; cuddling and closeness are usually reacted to with signs of pleasure. The gratifying response to contact with a soft object is illustrated by the close attachment of the infant to a toy animal or a blanket. It is also interestingly illustrated by studies of the baby monkeys provided with a "cloth mother."[1] The young monkeys would retreat to the protection of this soft object when lonely or frightened and under this "protection" would show expressions of increased satisfaction and courage.

We are familiar with the favorable response of infants to rocking and patting and particularly, of course, to the nipple or, as a substitute, the pacifier or the baby's own thumb.

Pleasurable sensations focused on the genitals become apparent early and are indicated by infantile masturbation. The infant's satisfactions gained from sucking his thumb, cuddling his toy animal or touching his genitals seem to have little specificity and he may alternate one or the other activity or correlate them as the opportunity presents itself. All of these activities tend nor-

[1]Harlow, H. F., and Zimmerman, R. R.: *Science, 130*:421, 1959.

mally to diminish in importance as the child grows older and turns his attention more away from his body and toward the outer world. He becomes engrossed in learning to walk, to manipulate objects and to communicate. He continues to some extent to make occasional use of autistic gratifications of this kind, but too persistent preoccupation with them indicates difficulties in socialization.

As the child becomes conscious of himself as boy or girl and, at the same time, conscious of more specific sexual excitation, he enters the so-called Oedipal[1] period of development to which we have already briefly referred. This period, covering variably ages three to seven, is a kind of "practice" period of sexual maturation.

The child during these years develops attachments to each parent individually. With increase in his social awareness he becomes cognizant of the close relationship between the parents and he may interpret that as a threat to his own secure relationship with either parent. Regardless of the sex of the child, this problem is initially most marked in relation to the mother. The tendency, however, is for the girl to shift her major emotional involvement to the father, while the boy's involvement persists most strongly with the mother. The resolution of these conflicts is accompanied by an increase in the capacities of the child for group socialization. This is achieved through a painful process by which the child must learn to deal with simultaneous mixed and opposite feelings. Such ambivalent feelings are a source of anxiety to the child for several reasons. The development of angry wishes toward a parent and for desire for the elimination of that parent — even if only in respect to this particular conflict — places the child in the center of a dilemma since he loves and needs both parents. Furthermore, the development of a desire for eliminating the parent confronts the child with his own fears of retaliation. In view of the relative strength of the parent and his power over the child, retaliation by a parent is frightening because of its destructive potentialities.

As has been indicated, this critical age is also the critical age

---

[1]The Oedipal concept gets its name from the myth of the Greek king, Oedipus who, through error, killed his father and married his mother.

for the development of identity. Physical aspects of oneself, such as the nature of the genitals, are strongly tied in to the self concept of the child. It is thus understandable that the child sees retaliative hostility from others as involving the destruction of crucial aspects or portions of himself or herself. The term "castration anxiety" and "castration complex" have been used to describe these fears and their projections into later life. Identification with the parent of the same sex is usually a positive element in the resolution of this Oedipal struggle. This is a critical period of interpersonal relationship for the child, and if it is not satisfactorily resolved it may result in permanent warping of the capacities for good mature love relationships.* Under normal circumstances, the child's fantasy and behavior gradually change from their infantile patterns. Internal controls develop and the character structure becomes better stabilized.

The child's problem is to recognize and accept his own place in the family. This is made difficult if there is too great seduction or too great rejection on the part of either parent. The typical neurotic Oedipal situation is that of the boy who remains closely tied to his mother, hostile toward and fearful of his father. He develops, as a result, competitive and anxious feelings about all masculine authority figures and an unsureness of his own capacities for sexual and aggressive activity. This unsureness of masculine identity may develop in a sensitive boy with an intimidating or inaccessible father and an over-protective mother. It may also occur in families where the father is very weak and the mother dominating, so that the boy lacks the satisfactory male identification figure. Similar conflicting feelings are exhibited by the girl who retains an intense attachment to her father with jealous rivalry of the mother.

The persistence of Oedipal fixations into adult life results in inhibitions of normal sexual development and/or distortions in one's self concept. There may be an attempt to find the parent through marriage to a motherly wife or a fatherly husband, usually with unsatisfactory results. Frequently seen is a dichotomy of attitudes as the result of which the person separates those

---

*Bosselman, B. C.: Castration anxiety and phallus envy, a reformulation. *Psychiat. Quart.*, 34:252, 1960.

of opposite sex into two groups: the sexual persons who are depreciated but physically desirable, and the nonsexual persons who are admired but are sexually taboo. This dichotomy has often been described in the male but is also not uncommon in the female. It makes for difficulties in marriage because a split feeling of this kind interferes with the integration of companionship and sexual satisfaction in a deeply fulfilling love relationship.

The child who feels unable to deal with the intense feelings of the Oedipal period may repress his sexual interests and remain fixed in an earlier pattern of dependency and rebellion toward adults. The oral (needful of support) and the anal (resistive to authority) struggles may predominate. We say he remains at a pregenital level of development.

Strongly repressed sexual feelings may, however, come out in exaggerated or distorted ways. The child, instead of progressing into the relatively sexually-latent next period of development may retain a preoccupation with sexual curiosity and exploration to a degree that interferes with his use of resources for other areas of interest. We will later observe that a child obsessed with guilty and anxious sexual thoughts may be inhibited in learning, either because his attention is too completely absorbed by these thoughts or because his guilt over these curiosities may spread out to inhibit all curiosities and he is afraid to learn. Attempts of these children to over-compensate for their anxiety by heterosexual or homosexual acting-out or by exhibitionism, peeping and the like, sets up a vicious circle of maladjustment. The parents respond severely to this behavior and this increases the child's guilt and fear and hence intensifies his need to further reassure himself by more acting-out.

Adult symptoms of frigidity, impotence and family discord are most commonly found to be based on sexual immaturity that originated in unhealthy early parent-child relationships.

As has been pointed out, the child's developmental problem is not merely one of sexuality per se, but involves a more inclusive concept of one's self as a boy or girl, as a man or woman. The male must feel boyish or manly and the female girlish or womanly, if they are to fit comfortably into the social pattern.

There is a complicated interaction of constitutional and environmental factors which make any individual masculine or feminine after the prevailing pattern. Not all boy babies are, by nature, aggressive and dominant, not all girl babies passive and receptive. Nor is the family environment necessarily conducive to the development of these traits. Parents who are disappointed in a child's sex may either deliberately or unconsciously push the child into the opposite role. The father encourages the little girl in activities that identify her with him, as sports and outdoor tasks; the mother may over-protect the boy and involve him in her interests. If the child's constitutional resources are sufficiently well differentiated, he may resist these influences, but if the boy is weak and timid, or the girl husky and awkward, they may develop a great deal of uncertainty as to their sexual identities.

As children mature they may attempt in various ways to deal with their uncertainties as to their sexual adequacy. One attempt is by over-compensation. The man constantly must prove his masculinity in a Don Juan type of behavior, denying his doubts by asserting his desirability as a sexual male. The woman who becomes a "frigid coquette" must prove her attractiveness to men over and over.

Compulsive behavior of this kind does not permit development of a lasting, mutually affectionate relationship with another person. Over-compensation also may express itself in non-sexual ways. The man who longs to be dependent and protected denies these longings in behavior that is dictatorial, tyrannical, compulsively active. The woman who desires an independent, active role presents herself as a passive, self sacrificing martyr. In these cases, the person's presentation of himself is very different from the person he really is.

In other cases, a tendency to identification with the opposite sex may be acted out within the limits of social acceptance. The man may marry a strong woman to take care of him; he may have a series of "illnesses"which make his dependence allowable. The masculine woman may assume dominance within the family and community.

These departures from the accepted type of behavior do not necessarily affect the sexual function per se. The person may deviate from the accepted pattern and still function heterosexually.

When the deviant orientation is so complete as to involve sexual feelings and behavior, the result is homosexuality.

Adult homosexuals will often say they have had feelings characteristic of the opposite sex as long as they can remember. The woman recalls never enjoying dolls or household tasks or pretty clothes and the man will tell of having been disinterested in sports, preferring girls' games and activities. Some believe that there is a predisposition involved, though it is not evident in any clearly defined physical deviation. Not all "sissies" are physical weaklings, though weakness may tend to favor a reaction of this kind. The "tomboy" may be quite feminine in somatic structure.

The question of constitutional determination is, of course, difficult to ascertain because of the effect on the child of the earliest environmental conditioning. Some female homosexuals will give a history of having a mother who was so depreciated and masochistic that the girl turned away from identification with her. Others will describe a sadistic, brutal father who made affectionate and sexual contact with the opposite sex seem frightening. The male often describes a weak, ineffectual father and a strong mother with whom he identified himself. Others seem to have formed a kind of submissive "inverted Oedipal" attachment to the father. It is as though they were so threatened by competition with the father that they capitulated to him and assumed a passive, dependent, "feminine" role.

R. T., a boy of fourteen, was referred for psychiatric study by the father who said, mysteriously, that the boy had told him he is "queer." The father, a successful, driving man, seemed to have little concern about the boy's feelings. He expressed a good deal of disappointment in him and worry about what people would think. The boy was a rather effeminate appearing, self-absorbed child. He told of having been seduced by older boys since he was thirteen. He said he had mixed feelings about these relationships, and he expressed interest also in girls. He said he had never felt close to either parent.

The mother was described as a cold, remote woman who had had several episodes of depression. An older brother was aggressive and successful like the father.

R. said that he felt all sexual feeling was bad. He did not

seem to be able to integrate it with respect and affection.

P. L., a sixteen-year-old girl, had always been a "tomboy," interested in sports and ambitious to be a physical education teacher. She had not been considered to be a problem until it was discovered that she had written a "love letter" to another girl, and the school referred her for psychiatric examination. P. admitted romantic interest in girls, but said she had had no overt homosexual experience. She had always preferred boys' activities, such as sports and cars, and was bored with domestic matters. She disliked feminine clothing, preferring shirts and slacks, and she wore her hair short. She said she had never had any sexual interest in boys and became irritated if they made any advances to her.

P. was the middle of three sisters. Her father had always encouraged her masculine interests. He was a dominating, tyrannical man. Her mother was a submissive, martyr-type of woman whom the children pitied. Two of the sisters had, however, established a closer relationship with the mother than P. had done. P. was considered to be "father's girl."

It was recommended that this girl be treated by a female therapist with whom she might establish a feminine identification. The homosexual orientation here was early established, and prognosis was considered to be doubtful.

It is important that the parents recognize these early manifestations and deviations in sexual identity because insofar as they are the result of intra-family relationships it may be possible to bring about some modifications in them. If they continue into adolescence and the child's sexual fantasies become attached to people of the same sex, the homosexual pattern may become irreversible.

Homosexuals fall into two groups,[1] according to the completeness of their deviation. The so-called constitutional or very early-conditioned pattern represents a general orientation characteristic of the opposite sex. The male homosexual of this type thinks and feels like a female and wants to be treated like one; the female has the outlook and the feelings of a male and is aggressive in her sexual approach. Deviation is usually quite obvious, being reflected in mannerisms, dress, overt interests.

[1]Carey, D.: *The Homosexual in America.* New York, Greenberg, 1951.

In contrast are the people who prefer homosexual relationships but still remain, in appearance and attitude, representative of their own sex. In this group, the original sexual identification seems to be normal but the individual develops a blocking at the genital level. A man, though he feels like a man, cannot have sexual interest in women, and the woman, though she is otherwise feminine, is unable to have sexual interest in a man.

These latter inhibitions seem to be closely related to difficulties in the Oedipal period which cause the child to retreat from heterosexual attachments and to seek substitution for it in emotionally-charged attachment to people of the same sex. It is a less diffuse deviation and hence more amenable to treatment. In many cases, the blocking is not complete and the individual may be able to become attached to "just the right kind" of person of opposite sex—presumably one who does not arouse a strong incest tabu. The man, for example, may accept a heterosexual relationship with a boyish-acting girl, and a woman may establish a companionable relationship with a not too sexually demanding man. The direction they go is determined partly by adult experience. Unfortunately, these borderline homosexuals are often seduced by those of the other group and have little opportunity or courage to try to resolve their difficulties.

The overt homosexual's life is handicapped by insecurity and stigmatization. It would seem, therefore, that every effort should be made by the pediatrician and child psychiatrist to detect and treat the aberrations of childhood which seem to point in this direction. Such prophylactic attempts are difficult and hazardous for two reasons. First, the child with deviant character traits will not necessarily develop sexual deviations, and attempts to force him into the accepted boy or girl pattern may arouse serious confusions in him. Second, a certain amount of homosexual interest is normal in childhood and adolescence and is likely to be worked through. Serious concern over such relatively normal behavior may do more harm than good. It may reflect anxieties and conflicts in the parents.

It must be remembered that homosexual acts are sometimes merely experimental or the result of suggestion or intimidation. If such acts are responded to with a great show of parental disapproval and shock, a child may develop a sense of guilt and shame which remains with him all his life.

Advice to the parents and approach to the child should, therefore, be attempted only with careful discrimination. There are, however, situations where the disturbance of identification seems quite clear and where there is a possibility of cooperation by the parent. In such cases, psychiatric treatment should be attempted. In a good relationship with a therapist, the child may be able to act out and overcome some of the fear and revulsion underlying his rejection of his sexual role.

SUMMARY

The child's sexual problems are concerned with, first: learning to deal realistically with his first sexual impulses and curiosities, and, second: forming a satisfactory concept of himself as a boy or a girl in terms of cultural expectations. The former problem is relatively simple and is largely influenced by the example and teaching of the parents. Sexual identification is a more complicated problem, contributed to constitution, to some extent, but to a large extent by identification with the parents. The girl who is unsure of her acceptability as a female, and the boy who doubts his masculinity, are prone to more or less serious social maladjustment in adult life, particularly involving close love relationships. Difficulties of this kind are often noticeable in early childhood.

SUGGESTED READINGS

Bieber, I. et al.: *Homosexuality.* New York, Basic Books, 1962.

Bornstein, B.: On latency. *Psychoanalytic Study of the Child, 6:*279, 1951.

Hampson, J. G., Money, J., and Hampson, S. L.: Hermaphroditism: Recommendations concerning case management. *J. Clin. Endocrinol. and metab., 16:*541, 1956.

Money, J., Hampson, J. G., and Hampson, S. L.: An examination of some basic sexual concepts: The evidence of human Hermaphroditism. *Bull. Johns Hopkins Hosp., 97:*301, 1955.

Money, J., Hampson, J. G., and Hampson, S. L.: Hermaphroditism: Recommendations concerning assignment of sex, change of sex, and psychologic management. *Bull. Johns Hopkins Hosp., 97*:284, 1955.

Thomas, R., Folkart, L., and Model, E.: The search for a sexual identity. *Psychoanalytic Study of the Child, XVIII*:636, 1963.

Pavenstedt, E.: The effect of extreme passivity imposed on a boy in early childhood, *Psychoanalytic Study of Child,* 2:396, 1946.

Erikson, E. H.: The problem of ego identity, *Jour. Am. Psychoanalytic Ass'n., IV,* 1956.

Chapter VI

Disturbances in Socialization and Learning

THE CHILD's earliest impressions of himself and of the world determine his way of life. They are the foundations on which his personality structure is built. Doubt, fear and distrust impair self-reliance and favor a rigid, defensive kind of behavior which may create a great many difficulties in social integration. The study of children can reveal more clearly than can the study of adults the origins of such behavior patterns. For example, we can often see in pediatric practice the child whose development in some areas is retarded or who, after reaching a certain stage of development, returns to a more infantile stage. These phenomena are known as fixation and regression. A child of six who continues to suck his thumb or who remains enuretic is remaining fixed at a more infantile way of functioning. A child of this age who has been thoroughly toilet trained and who begins to wet the bed or to soil in response to some increased environmental difficulty is regressing to an earlier stage of development.

One of the commonest causes of regressive behavior is the birth of a sibling. The older child, feeling deprived and displaced, competes with the unwelcome infant by making increased demands on the mother for attention. If his behavior is understood and wisely dealt with he need not, of course, suffer any lasting damage. However, it is not uncommon to find neurotic character traits in adults which began as regressive reactions of sibling rivalry.

The child who clings to the dependency of infancy may develop learning difficulties. The energies which should be involved in mastering the environment through learning are, instead, inhibited by the child's primitive impulses. He is self-absorbed, confused in his relationships with his parents, afraid and/or unwilling to renounce dependency to a point of assuming an active, responsible approach. His failure to learn may be contributed to

82

by discouragement by the parents or it may be the result of too great expectations and pressure by the parents. In the first instance, the child's attempts at self-expression and at achievement have been so harshly criticized that he is afraid to try anything new. In the second case, he feels that his parents expect him to do well for them and in hostile rebellion he resists giving them this satisfaction.

The aspect of the personality which is directly concerned in the learning process is referred to as the ego. We have already described perceiving and integrating ego functions. One may speak of ego energies as being directed toward dealing with the realities of the outer world, while at the same time making internal adaptations between the primitive impulses, often referred to as id-impulses, and the internalized social attitude sometimes referred to as superego. Adaptation to the environment necessitates such important ego functions as observing, remembering and organizing. Hartman* suggests that there are some primary autonomous ego capacities at birth. These are reinforced and extended in the process of maturation. Such extensions of primary ego capacities are associated with the elaboration of secondary autonomous ego functions: the late developing ego aspects of the character. Success in this learning process requires, of course, the inborn capacity for observation, retention and analysis which we call intelligence. One's intelligence is the tool of his ego. But success requires also that the energies of the ego be free for learning. The child whose energies are too completely absorbed in internal struggles cannot apply himself successfully to mastering the realities about him. His emotional state of conflict interferes.

Excessive repression of sexual curiosity may interfere with the learning process. The child has questions about his origin and an interest in anatomical differences. If his attempts to learn in this area are strongly suppressed he may react by more intense preoccupation with the subject. This may engage him to the extent of interfering with learning attempts in other directions. Also, he may be so intimidated by the rebuffs of his sexual curiosity that

*Hartman, H.: Ego Psychology and the Problem of Adaptation. New York, International Universities Press, 1958.

he represses excessively other curiosities as well, as though he were afraid that learning would be punished.

> A. N., a boy of eight and the child of a progressive, ambitious family, came in with the report of being unable to learn, although he had a high I.Q. In school he seemed preoccupied and unable to concentrate. He did a great deal of day dreaming. The child's parents were very permissive with their children, and particularly permissive in allowing the children to see the parents nude and in bed. The mother was a sexually provocative woman with her boy, and it seemed apparent that the child needed to deny any interest in the sexual stimulation. In doing this he denied interest, in general, in the world about him and retreated into day dreams.
>
> The parents in their discussion with the psychiatrists were made aware of what they were doing to their children and they cooperated well in trying to be less provocative with them. After a few months of changed attitude on the part of the parents the child showed improvement in his school activity, indulged less in day dreams and was able to apply himself to his studies.

The drives to learn must be sufficiently disassociated from the strivings for dependency satisfaction and infantile sexual satisfaction so that they can flow freely outward to cope with the continually challenging problems of living.

Just as the child's attitudes toward feeding are strongly influenced by the people who feed him, so his concepts of learning are affected by those who teach him. Often the expectations of the parent are reflected in the kind of motivations a child develops. He may work hard to learn, but largely to prove his superiority (and to prove to his parents that they have a superior child). As long as he is praised and rewarded for achievement, he will function well, but he is working under tension and without sufficient joy in learning for its own sake. Such a child reacts poorly to failure or to lack of praise. Motivation of this kind may have in it a strong element of hostility. "I'll show them!" or "I'll show the others (often siblings) how stupid they are!"

> A boy of fifteen, R. N., came for psychiatric consultation on the advice of his parents. He had dropped out of high school

where he was doing failing work.

The boy's father was a research worker and an outstandingly scholarly man. An older sister had a brilliant school record. Younger brothers, aged ten and four, got most of the mother's attention.

The patient's school history was that he had attended many progressive schools in many parts of the country, as his father had traveled from one campus to another a great deal. The boy had never concentrated well on his studies and had been interested in applying himself only to those subjects which came easily to him. He seemed to need immediate success and he liked to talk in a profound way about such subjects as English literature, though he completely rejected mathematical and scientific studies.

Etiologic factors here were the family's extreme interest in academic success and disregard of the patient's emotional needs, the frequent moves of the family, the lack of structure in the progressive school system, and the feeling of discouragement in trying to compete with the older sister. The boy's resistances were so extreme that it was finally decided to send him to a school for disturbed children where, with intensive psychiatric care, he was gradually able to improve his study habits.

It is often observed that if one child of a family is being praised as an achiever, a jealous sibling reacts in an opposite direction and refuses to compete. He neglects his studies and assumes an "I don't care" attitude as though to depreciate the strivings of his successful sibling.

Parents should help children to find a joy in learning for its own sake and to see it also in terms of social usefulness, rather than as a weapon of competition. Willingness to answer the child's questions, to share his interests and to stimulate him from time to time with new interests are characteristics of parents which create a favorable milieu for learning.

H. G. was a seven-year-old girl who had not attended school. When she was five years old, the mother and she went to kindergarten and the child refused to be separated from her mother. She cried all of the first day of kindergarten and refused to go to school the second day. The mother, therefore, decided not to enroll her at that time. When she was six the process was repeated. After crying all day, for the first three days of the school year, the school authorities had the child sit in the principal's office for two additional days of crying. Following this, she was sent back home. The parents were informed that they should bring her back the following year.

This referral came in September of her seventh year of life when it was discovered that the same pattern was being maintained. With the exception of this presented problem, the patient was a charming, sweet child. She tended to get along well with people and seemed quite bright. In spite of not having attended school, she had picked up all the skills of the first grade, and, in many respects, was well in advance of her age. This was understandable, for the mother devoted much of her time to tutoring the child and compensating for her absence from school.

The father was a very successful businessman who had not had very much time for his child. Both parents freely admitted that the mother had "devoted her life" to this daughter. She stated that her life really began to take on meaning at the birth of her daughter. At that time her circle of friends narrowed to consist largely of other women in the neighborhood with children of a similar age. From the time the patient was three, she and her mother had talked about school a great deal and the patient had early expressed a feeling that she wanted to go to school. Both parents were at a loss to explain her resistance. The mother tells of what a good child the patient was, causing absolutely no trouble. She "went everywhere that mother went." According to the father, the mother and daughter were inseparable. The mother admitted she felt very bad for a week or two each time the child was unable to attend school but that, following this, she settled down and became comfortable and proceeded to teach the child the things that she lost by not attending school.

Following diagnostic evaluation it was decided that the child must go to school and that the mother would be treated. The mother had derived much gratification from her child's presence and really had very strongly mixed feelings about allowing the child to go to school. Although on the one hand she favored the child's development, she was also unconsciously anticipating the emptiness in her life in the child's absence. The little girl shared and responded to these feelings.

The acute phobic reactions were seen as the child's response to the impending separation from the mother. After a few psychiatric interviews, the child was persuaded to start at school. She was somewhat withdrawn from the other children for one week and subsequent to this had no difficulty. An effort was made to explain to the mother some of the problems she had relative to her child. She began to realize that she had been using this girl to fill a gap in her life which actually had originated in terms of her feeling of lack of relationship with her own mother. She said, "I don't want my daughter ever to experience the distance from her mother which I had with mine."

As she was able to establish a less intense relationship with her daughter, she turned more to her husband and he, in turn, spent more time at home. A follow-up, three years after the termination of the treatment, indicated that the child was apparently well-adjusted at school and the family situation seemed relatively stable.

Once the child enters school, the responsibility for his progress is shared with the teacher and with the school system. Unfortunately, this system is too often highly competitive and also allows little time for individual pupil problems. A sensitive, perceptive teacher who can establish a good rapport with her class may function well in spite of crowded classrooms and emphasis on grades. Many adults look back with gratitude to a relationship with such a teacher. Many others, however, recall traumatic school experiences which warped their attitudes toward learning for years or, sometimes, for life.

A child who truants excessively, who refuses to go to school, or who exhibits an intense anxiety in relation to attendance, may be having realistic problems with his teacher or his schoolmates. On the other hand, he may be merely projecting into the school situation fears and hostilities that are only secondarily related to it.

We have already discussed some of the poorly socialized reactions of the child which result from a too-passive or too-impulsive approach. He withdraws into a solitary, daydreaming existence or he acts out violently without regard for the rights and welfare of other people.

There are other types of reactions which may become habitual and may act as handicaps to good social integration. One such reaction pattern is projection: the tendency to place the blame for difficulties on someone or something outside one's self, rather than to face one's own responsibilities. This tendency leads to a paranoid type of behavior which can be destructive both to the individual and, under some circumstances, also to the object of his blame.

Paranoia begins when the child defends himself against punishment by projecting blame for his own offenses. "I didn't do it; brother did," or "It wasn't my fault; the teacher lied." Such projections are more prevalent, of course, among children who have reason to fear punishment by their parents; however, children under the best of circumstances find this a useful mechanism of defense at times. If it is excessively used, it can lead to a suspicious, "chip on shoulder" attitude toward other people which makes a child quarrelsome and antagonistic, and causes others to dislike him. Thus a vicious circle of social maladjustment is set up.

The child may project not only the blame for his behavior but also the feelings motivating that behavior. For example, the angry child assumes anger in others.

Paranoid attitudes may appear in the individual as a result of his particular difficulties in group integration and hence may set him apart in his group. In other cases, these attitudes may unite him with a group, the members of which agree in projecting accusations against a scapegoat of some kind. The solitary paranoid, whose distorted thinking labels him as eccentric or even as mentally deranged, is an unhappy, ineffectual person but, in most cases, he is not a serious threat to society. When, however, the paranoid potentialities in human nature are intensified by group solidarity under demagogic leadership, the result is often horrifying.

No person is born paranoid, though some babies exhibit more irritability and less affectionate responsiveness than others. Such children would require less trauma to develop a suspicious, hostile, projective personality than would the more passive and affectionate infants. However, severe emotional deprivation has been shown to be clearly related. Rene Spitz* in his studies of babies reared in institutions without mothering care and affection, found that in many cases they developed a suspicious, irritable attitude toward people which became a firmly established personality characteristic.

The child who is vulnerable to paranoid thinking shows early indications of suspiciousness and tendency to blame others for his difficulties. These tendencies in him may reflect similar attitudes of his family. Some parents encourage their children to be distrustful of other people. They will side with the child against his teachers and his playmates, insisting always that no blame is his. Such early conditioning to projection may create a vicious circle of maladjustment. The child becomes a poor sport, he is therefore disliked by others, and this intensifies his feelings of being discriminated against. However, a bright and active child may resist parental attitudes of this kind and not be seriously influenced by them. It is the child who feels weak and unsure of himself who will take over paranoid family attitudes in order to avoid a sense of failure.

Such direct conditioning is not necessarily present in the history of a paranoid person. Children may use the projective mechanism not as a reflection of a family pattern but as a defense against the family. The parent, instead of siding with the child, may blame him excessively, may be intolerant and rejecting of him. In reaction, he tries frantically to avoid their criticism by the simple expedient of shifting the blame. In a critical atmosphere of this kind, distrust and concealment are prevalent. The child dare not confide in his parents because he feels they are not "for" him. If he has relatives or other friendly adults to whom he can turn for encouragement and support the effect of parental rejection may be minimized; otherwise a projective defense, once established, may well become his characteristic method of adaptation.

A paranoid woman in a mental hospital once remarked, "The words of a song keep running in my head: 'I'm just a little prairie flower growing wilder every hour. Nobody ever cultivated me.'"

*Spitz, R.: Psychoanalytic Study of the Child, Vol. 2. 1946, p. 312.
 Spitz, R.: *Internat. J. Psychoanalysis*, 31:1, 1950.

This lack of individual "cultivation" was characteristic of her life history.

An individual with paranoid ideas tends to be set apart, to live a relatively lonely life. He may be considered a bit "queer" and disagreeable, hard to get along with, but capable of working and presenting a normal facade. Such a person is vulnerable to a psychotic breakdown if his life situation becomes too intolerable to him. In a paranoid schizophrenic distortion of reality he then allows himself to feel the power and significance which he lacks in reality.

We have observed that paranoid ideas are aimed at externalizing impulses or ideas which originate endogenously but which are recognized as unacceptable to others, or to the person himself. "This is not I; this is something done to me," relieves the guilt and fear of retribution which would otherwise be felt by the individual having such impulses or ideas. In this way the process resembles that of phobia formation in which internal conflict is externalized and symbolized. The phobic patient who fears and avoids knives is thus fearing and avoiding his own hostile impulses.

There is also, in paranoid thinking, a kind of dissociation similar to that which we will observe on a physiologic basis in conversion hysteria. The patient with the hysterical paralysis of the leg has "cut off" that leg and reacts physically as if it were not a part of his organism. Similarly, a psychotic idea of persecution is cut off from the normal processes of logical thinking. This idea is impervious to rational perception and logical reasoning.

Obviously, projection as a method of adaptation is unconstructive both for the individual and for the social group. Once established, it is very difficult to treat. It follows, therefore, that attitudes in the family and cultural milieu which contribute to its genesis in the child should be recognized by those in professional relationships with the child: his doctor, teacher, pastor, group leader and, possibly, social worker and school psychologist. The lonely, suspicious, hostile child is reacting to a hostile, often highly competitive environment. He needs to learn to trust and, in so doing, to dare to accept responsibility for his own behavior.

Another reaction pattern which is of universal occurrence but may be exaggerated to the point of pathology is over-compensation. By this is meant the concealment of an inappropriate impulse by an extreme reaction in an opposite direction. The wish to be dependent is denied by a fanatically overly active attitude; extreme interest in sex is covered by prudery; hostile, rebellious feelings by an outward show of meekness; and, in contrast, fearfulness lies underneath bragging and bullying behavior.

As the child matures he develops an ego ideal, a more or less unconscious image of himself as he wants to be. When his impulses are not consistent with this image he may deny them, even to himself, and in fighting off these impulses, may overreact. This kind of over-compensatory behavior has been described in a previous chapter as characteristic of neurotic compulsiveness. The compulsive person is rigid and very exact in behavior, perfectionistic according to his own standards, and unable to be relaxed and spontaneous. It is as though he must discipline himself to act according to a certain pattern, lest the repressed, unacceptable attitudes might be revealed. Under ordinary circumstances, the very young child expresses his impulses quite frankly and when he does try to conceal them by opposite reaction, the process is apparent. As he grows older, however, and is motivated more by the forces of guilt and shame, he sees himself as he wants to be and may deny vigorously the existence of character traits inconsistent with this self image.

We might stop briefly at this point to distinguish between guilt and shame, both of which play so large a part in determining personality structure.

Some authors define guilt as a sense of having offended against other people; shame as a sense of having offended against one's self. The former depends on the superego, the latter on the ego ideal.

We have already defined superego as the aspect of oneself which incorporates behavioral codes which have been gradually taken over from family and society as part of the process of developing an identity. The young child is motivated at first externally, behaving in ways which avoid punishment and win love and approval. Later his own sense of what is acceptable directs him. The primitive instinctual tendencies within him are modified according to these internal social principles. When his behavior is not in accord with these principles, he may experience guilty feelings, a feeling of loss of self-esteem, of being unworthy and unloved.

Shame need not imply an offense against social-moral codes. One feels shame at having performed poorly in an examination or having presented himself awkwardly on a social occasion. Shame is aroused by situations by which one loses face, feels a sense of loss of control and dignity. One may, however, also feel shame at having behaved unkindly or deceitfully toward others, in which case guilt and shame exist together. There is usually some overlapping of these concepts. However, in order to understand the disturbed reactions of children (as well as of adults) one should understand the distinctions between them.

The child who has been strongly disciplined through intimidation may develop a rigid moral sense based on the idea that wrongdoing leads to punishment. Even wrong thoughts and unacceptable wishes may create a sense of guilt in him. As we have observed in our discussion of aggression, intense repression of the aggressive and hostile impulses leads to a state of poor equilibrium. The rebellious thoughts and feelings that have been so sternly denied may come out indirectly or they may arouse such strong guilt that the child punishes himself in various ways. In other cases, as we have mentioned, these unacceptable impulses may be guarded against by compulsive, exact behavior.

An exacting ego ideal may develop under different circumstances, particularly in a milieu in which the children are highly regarded and much is expected of them.

SUMMARY

The social development of the child implies a progress from purely self-centered, self-gratifying motivations to motivations which also consider the welfare of other people. The child learns to give and take, to contribute as well as to demand. He comes to value deterrents which are abstract and idealized, which include such sentiments as loyalty, sympathy, group pride. If, because of poor resources and/or an extremely restricting, warping environment, the child does not develop this wider social perspective, his life remains narrow and full of conflict. He continues in an emotionally greedy, "oral" approach, isolated, yet needful. He is resistive to social demands, in fact, even to the demands which his own maturation makes on him. His retentive, resistive "anality" is expressed in negativism and a rigidly self-contained attitude. He is critical of others and expects that they are critical of him. He may be outwardly rebellious, even delinquent, or he may cover his rebellion with a compulsive facade of conformity. His orality keeps him dependent on others, without confidence in himself and unable to share. His immature superego remains based on the Talion Law of evil and punishment, rather than on the broader, more flexible principles of social interaction.

Obviously, any person's constitutional endowment contributes to his degree of success in social integration. Intelligence, energy, capacity for imaginative and abstract thinking, good homeostatic function, all influence the kind of adaptations that will be made. The physician cannot change the child's endowment. He can, however, work with the parents to bring about a greater awareness of the child's sensitivities to his environment. Any child will make the best use of his potentialities in a milieu which gives him the right balance of loving gratifications and consistent discipline, of protection and expectation. In a seriously damaging environment, even a well-equipped child will be handicapped in his attempts to live cooperatively and constructively with other people.

SUGGESTED READINGS

Ackerman, N. W.: *The Psychodynamics of Family Life.* New York, Basic Books, 1958.

Anthony, E. J.: The System-makers: Piaget and Freud, in *British J. Medical Psychology*, 30:255, 1957.

Anthony, E. J.: The Significance of Jean Piaget for Child Psychiatry, in *British J. Med. Psychology*, 29:20, 1956.

Blanchard, P.: Psychoanalytic contributions to the problems of reading disabilities, *Psychoanalytic Study of Child*, 2:163, 1947.

Bonney, M. C.: Parents as the makers of social deviates, *Soc. Forces*, 20:77, 1941.

Caplan, G.: *Emotional Problems of Early Childhood.* New York, Basic Books, 1959.

Cass, L. K.: Parent-child relationships and delinquency, *J. Abnormal and Social Psychol.*, 47:101, 1952.

Coolidge, J. et al.: Patterns of aggression in school phobia. *Psychoanalytic Study of the Child*, XVII:319, 1962.

Friedlander, K.: Neurosis and home background, *Psychoanalytic Study of Child*, III/IV, 1949.

Galdstone, I.: *The Family in Contemporary Society*, New York Academy Med., 1958.

Goldfarb, W.: *Childhood Schizophrenia.* Cambridge, Mass., Harvard Univ. Press, 1961.

Hartmann, H., and Lowenstein, R. M.: Notes on the superego. *Psychoanalytic Study of the Child*, XVII:42, 1962.

Johnson, A. M., et al.: School phobia. *Amer. Jour. Orthopsychiatry*, XI, 1941.

Lidz, T.: *The Family and Human Adaptation*, New York, International Univ. Press, 1963.

Lumpkin, K.: Parental conditions of Wisconsin girl delinquents, *Am. J. Sociol.*, 38:233, 1932.

Pearson, G. H. J.: A survey of learning difficulties in children, *Psychoanalytic Study of Child*, 7:322, 1952.

Rapaport, D.: *The Organization and Pathology of Thought.* New York, Columbia Univ. Press, 1951.

Rubin, Vera (Ed.): *Culture, Society and Health*, New York Acad. Sci., Dec., 1960.

Ruesch, W.: *Disturbed Communication*, New York, W. W. Norton, 1957.

Spitz, R. A.: On the genesis of superego components. *Psychoanalytic Study of the Child*, XIII:375, 1958.

Spock, B.: The striving for autonomy and regressive object relationships. *Psychoanalytic Study of the Child*, XVIII:361, 1963.

Tinbergen, N.: *The Study of Instinct,* Oxford, Clarendon Press, 1951.

Tinbergen, N.: *Social Behavior in Animals,* London, Methuen, 1953.

Waelder, R.: The structure of paranoid ideas, *International J. Psychoanalysis,* 32:167, 1951.

Chapter VII

The Hospitalized Child

In evaluating the development of a child, the focus of the physician is ordinarily on the individual in an office or clinic setting. The physician, of course, takes into consideration the presence of the parent and the interplay between the child and the parent during the interview and examination.

It must be recognized, however, that the setting for this type of examination is, in many respects, unique and artificial. Much in addition can be learned of the behavior of a child if he can be observed in his family, in his school, or in his play group. Unfortunately, observation in these environments is often not feasible for the physician.

The physician does, however, have the opportunity to observe some children in a hospital setting. The pediatric ward is not merely a place where children receive medical treatment. It has its own peculiar complex social structure and organization. The behavior of the child can be conveniently observed in this milieu. It is evident that the nature of the child's responses on the pediatric ward varies with his stage of development and, to a large extent, reflects the history of his previous adjustment in his family. Thus a study of the child in a dynamic hospital environment provides a basis for the physician to understand the adjustment of the child to other groups with either highly structured or loosely organized society. The reactions of the child in the hospital for medical illness also illustrate in a frank and exaggerated way, the feelings and attitudes which adult patients have but do not directly express, in a similar situation. In the child and in the adult the nature of the hospital adjustment is dependent primarily on the patient's basic personality structure.

Hospitalization is, for many children, a severely disturbing event which, under some circumstances, may distort the child's attitudes even irreversibly. The trauma varies greatly depending on the age of the child, the nature of his relationship with his parents and the capacity of the hospital to provide individualized substitute mothering. It depends also, of course, on the nature of his illness and the necessary medical and surgical manipulations involved.

Separation from the mother is generally anxiety-producing from the time the baby begins to recognize her as the important person in his life, at the age of about eight months. Studies have shown that separation anxiety increases from this time on and reaches a peak in children from eighteen to twenty-four months of age. After that it gradually diminishes as the child can come to comprehend the need for the separation and its temporary character. A realization of the severe impact of hospitalization on the eighteen to twenty-four-month-old child should influence the doctor's decision as to home versus hospital care.

Studies by Robertson, Bowlby, David, Nicolas and Roudinesco[1] have been devoted to the response of children of this vulnerable age to hospitalization. These investigators describe the emotional response of the child as progressing commonly through the phases of protest, despair and denial.

In the phase of protest, which may last from a few hours to a week, the child attempts to recapture his lost mother with the expectation that she will respond to his cry. The first behavior at this stage will consist of loud cries, shaking the crib, and looking expectantly toward any sign of the return of the mother. The phase of protest is followed by the phase of despair expressed in an attitude of hopelessness. The child at this stage is apathetic and withdrawn and makes no significant demands on the ward staff. The phase of denial follows the period of despair and is characterized by repression by the child of his emotional need for his mother. In part, the state of denial develops from the need of the child to satisfy his physical requirements for which he must have the aid of ward personnel. He may attach himself to a substitute mother figure on the ward. He may begin to act as if contact with maternal figures has little significance

[1]Roudinesco, J., David, M., and Nicolas, J.: in Courrier, *Centre Internationale de L'enfance,* II, 66 (1952); also Robertson, J. and Bowlby, J., in II, 131 (1952).

to him. This development may, in part, be the result of successive loss of maternal figures, resulting from the normal rotation of nurses in the course of regular duties or their transfer to other wards. In the stage of denial there may be an increased interest in toys and food as the apparent need for the mother declines.

A few children, even of this critical age group, accept hospitalization with apathy or apparent cheerfulness. In such cases, it is usually found that the child has not formed a strong attachment to any parent figure due to the absence or disinterest of such a person. He has learned to relate superficially to his environment with little individual preference, a personality trait which will persist into adult life. Therefore, though the docile and accepting hospital patient makes less trouble for the nursing staff and gives a superficial appearance of good adjustment, this is not a favorable reaction in a child who should presumably be at an age of close attachment to his parents.

It is obvious that unnecessary hospitalization of children should be avoided. The period of hospitalization should be curtailed to the minimum, and the efficiency of the performance of the necessary diagnostic procedures expedited. These cautions should be particularly kept in mind, as has already been noted, in relation to the child of the most vulnerable age.

If the child is old enough to understand, he should be informed of the hospitalization and its general purpose, shortly before coming to the institution. It may be helpful for the physician to coach the parents about this when hospital plans are being made. A child who is left in the hospital after being led to believe he is going elsewhere, will certainly be predisposed to distrust his parents. He should be reassured about the nature and the necessity for the action, and one or both of his parents should accompany him to the ward. A toy or some other treasured possession from home is often comforting.

In most primitive cultures the mother refuses to be separated from her sick child and the entire family may move into the hospital to care for the child. It has been reported that in such cultures (in spite of the higher prevalent death rate among children) the child appears to be less traumatized by hospitalization.

The young infant who has not as yet established a strong

emotional attachment to individuals may soon accept the hospital surroundings and behave much as he did at home.

It is evident that the traumatic effect of hospitalization and maternal separation are less severe in the child over two years of age because he has a better capacity to comprehend hospitalization as a temporary interlude, rather than as a great disaster, and to tolerate the ego-stress. Also, he has achieved a greater degree of independence of his parents.

Older children who are not acutely ill may soon become adjusted to the hospital and become engaged in play activity. Much of the activity may fall into a semi-organized pattern of ward society with patient leadership demonstrated by the older and more intelligent children. Some of the children, by virtue of a long stay on the ward, are so familiar with the routines that there is no demonstrable anxiety in response to the constant changes of ward personnel. Children who are adjusted but who have been hospitalized more recently will exhibit the normal childhood curiosity with regard to their surroundings.

This routine pattern of ward activity is periodically disturbed by the necessity of the staff to perform certain painful procedures on the children in accordance with their need for medical care. These children will accept the need for recurrent phyical examination ordinarily without great protest and with minimal disturbance to the ward. Such procedures as the drawing of blood or the painful changes of dressing arouse obvious displeasure in the patient, accompanied by vigorous crying. Following the procedure, however, the child usually falls back into the pattern of ward behavior. Little or no sympathy is shown by the other children toward the child subjected to these procedures but after they are completed the child is quickly welcomed back into the group activity.

Children who are acutely ill are seldom disturbed by the remainder of the ward patients. The acutely ill child will undergo a defensive regression and will either pass the time with no organized activity or engage in simple play by himself or with his visiting parents.

The orderly type of activity is temporarily disturbed by the arrival of a new admission to the ward. The child aged two or older usually follows a typical pattern of behavior on admission. He will cling to his parents and frequently will cry vigorously, voicing objections to the need for a stay in the hospital and asking to return home. Attention by ward nurses and other personnel is greeted with suspicion and hostility. Examination by a physician may be tolerated despite overt signs of anger, but there may be active resistance to the more unpleasant parts of the examination. The departure of the parents is usually the signal for a protest by the child. After the parents have left, the intensity of crying diminishes but the general rejection of ward personnel and other patients continues. Food may be rejected, and play articles refused. A child will tend to continue this behavior until he falls asleep. By the next morning, he will ordinarily react more favorably to the relief of his basic needs by ward nurses and aids. He begins to fall into the pattern of play activity consistent with his age, and finds his way into ward society. This process may occur very quickly or it may take several days. If hospitalization is followed by rapid improvement in well-being, such as that accompanying the response of a respiratory infection to antibiotics, ward adjustment will be expedited. If hospitalization is necessitated by an acute painful illness or if it leads to surgical procedures, the period of adaptation to the ward will naturally be prolonged.

The overt manifestations of the child on hospitalization reflect his anxiety with regard to separation from his parents plus the potential threat of the hospital and its procedures. Similar behavior is observed in his own home, when he is left in the hands of a strange baby sitter as the parents leave for the evening. It is to be anticipated that in the face of illness, which ordinarily causes a reversion to more infantile types of behavior, and in the face of strange surroundings of a hospital the emotional reaction induced by separation from the parents will be intensified.

The child's previous experiences determine, to a large extent, his ability to cope with this new traumatic situation. Experiences which have made him unsure of his parents and distrustful of adults in general create an unfavorable mental set in him. If, however, he has a sound relationship with his parents it is relatively easier for him to establish quickly a similar relationship with parental figures in the hospital. Much can be done by the hospital staff to expedite this adjustment. Frequent visits by the parents also contribute to a good outcome.

Visiting hours on pediatric wards previously took place for an hour, two or three times a week. These were trying periods for the children, the parents and the hospital staff. The child, at the onset of the visiting hour, would respond in many instances with either excessive dependency or with overt hostility. His anger toward his parents for deserting him and leaving him would be expressed by ignoring them, rejecting their gifts, or by crying. The end of the visiting hour, often signaled by the ringing of a bell or a buzzer, would set off violent protests. A good deal of the emotional difficulty related to visiting hours has been avoided in the modern hospital by prolonging visiting hours for all children, by allowing daily visiting and permitting unlimited visiting for the parents of the children who are extremely ill or in need of an unusual amount of emotional support.

Surgery is a terrifying experience for any child, and good presurgical preparation is especially important. The helplessness of the child relative to the adult, his lack of understanding of the need for treatment, the difficulty of the staff in communicating with the patient, and the anxiety of the parents, all contribute to a situation in which an upset state cannot be considered abnormal. Some of the fear can be alleviated by a sympathetic but honest and matter-of-fact discussion with the child. The presurgical use of sedatives is, of course, a great help.

The sick child sometimes becomes aware of the reality of death in the hospital group and of its potential threat to his own existence. His usual method of defense is denial as seen by his exclusion of the morbid patient from the social group and his lack of reference to children who have just died. This is probably the best defense of which young children are capable, and any attempt to encourage verbalization of feeling may only upset and confuse them. If a child occasionally asks a question or seeks to reach out for reassurance from nurses or physicians, he should of course be encouraged to talk and be given comfort and assisted in the process of strengthening his denial defenses.

The pediatric ward itself is less frightening if designed with a decor suitable for children and not appearing as a smaller version of an adult ward. Small tables and chairs, small toilets and work stands, and adequate play areas away from bed are a necessity. The child should usually be permitted to be out of bed and active in ward activity as soon as he is well enough.

It is fortunate indeed if the ward is staffed by personnel who include mature women emotionally able to play a maternal role to their patients. Sufficient time must be available for them to get acquainted with the children, to call them by name and develop some awareness of their individual problems. Such relationships help a great deal in overcoming the child's loneliness and fear.

As has already been implied, visiting hours should be daily and for long periods, preferably in the afternoon. Parents should be encouraged to come and help in the care of the child when possible. It is especially important that the child awakening from an anesthetic should have his mother present as he regains consciousness if this is at all feasible.

Psychiatric consultation should be routinely available in managing the problems of a children's service. Children in particular need of such study include not only the very aggressively protesting ones but, even more, those who seem apathetic, withdrawn and self-absorbed or overly fearful and anxious. The consultant in such cases may establish helpful collaboration with the social service department of the hospital. The social worker should have knowledge of the family relationships and be able to contribute to an understanding of the child's reactions. She also may, in some cases, be able to talk with the parents and help them to deal wisely with their child's disturbed behavior.

For children who must remain for any length of time in a hospital, the institution becomes a small community. Besides the ward's doctors, nurses and aids, the patients may have contact with occupational therapists, teachers, physical therapists and social workers. The list is sometimes supplemented by medical students, student nurses and volunteer workers. Such numerous contacts may bewilder the small patient unless he can attach himself securely and reliably to one or two of the people around him: hopefully a staff member who is in constant daily attendance. It is very important that he find a familiar and constant figure in the group on whom he can depend for comfort and support.

The pediatric hospital can never be an adequate substitute to the child for his own home. However, if its general atmosphere is homelike, and if the staff provides considerate and individualized care, the degree of psychological trauma will be minimized.

The after-effects of hospitalization on a child of vulnerable age may be quite persistent and may take various forms. When his parents take him home he may at first seem irritable and angry, tending to be negativistic and unresponsive to demonstrations of affection. He may, on the other hand, express his anxiety in an opposite way by clinging to the mother, following her about and indicating great apprehension in her absence. A third type of reaction is that of a child who seems indifferent and withdrawn from his parents as though afraid to allow himself to be attached to them again. All these acute reactions may give way after a few days to a state of generalized emotional upset in which the child weeps bitterly for no apparent reason. He seems to be exhibiting a delayed expression of the grief and fear which he suppressed during his period of separation.

It is important that the parents understand what is happening when they bring their child home from the hospital and that they respond with patience and reassurance. Under these circumstances, as the child accepts the fact that he is again secure with his parents his unstable behavior should gradually disappear. If, however, the trauma has been severe, and/or the parents are lacking in understanding, the disturbed attitude may become a part of the child's developing character structure.

The doctor tends to feel that his duties are fulfilled once he has treated the sick child and discharged him from the hospital. Some follow-up discussions with the parents concerning the readjustment problems may, however, in the long run be fully as important as good medical care.

The principles of our analysis of the problems of the hospitalized child can be extended to apply to the child at school, to the child in a play group, to the child at church, to the child at camp and to the child in a changing family setting. In each instance, the nature of the interplay is dependent on the previous experience and personality development of the child and upon the social structure of the group. In the course of the interaction the individual changes to some extent but his basic personality development is still largely determined by his initial experiences in his family.

SUMMARY

In considering whether or not to hospitalize a sick child, the physician must take into account the effect of separation from the parents, particularly in a child younger than two years. When hospitalization is necessary, the child should be prepared for it, insofar as he is able to comprehend, by an honest and simple discussion with him of the plan. Frequent visits by parents, and individualized attention by a constant member of the hospital staff help to minimize the child's separation anxiety. Post-hospital reactions of children occur frequently, and the parents should be prepared to understand them and to deal patiently with them. Psychiatric and social service consultations may be indicated in the case of children whose reactions to hospitalization suggest serious trauma and poor ego defenses. The social experience of the child in the hospital should be within a family-like unit, rather than with a multi-shift personnel structure patterned after industrial organizations.

SUGGESTED READINGS

Blum, G. E.: The reaction of hospitalized children to illness. *Pediatrics, XXII*:590, 1958.

Calef, V.: Psychological consequences of physical illness in childhood. *Jour. Am. Psychoanalytic Ass'n., XII*, 1959.

Jessner, L. and Kaplan, S.: Observations on the Emotional Reactions of Children with Tonsillectomy and Adenoidectomy, *Problems of Infancy and Childhood*, Senn, M. J. (Ed.), New York, Josiah Macy Foundation, 1948.

Levy, D.: Psychic trauma of operations in children, and a note on combat neurosis, *Am. J. of the Disturbed Child, LXIX*:7, 1945.

Lipton, S. D.: On the psychology of childhood tonsilectomy, *Psychoanalytic Study of Child*, 17:363, 1962.

Nagy, M. H.: The Child's View of Death, in Ferfel, H. (Ed.): *The Meaning of Death*, New York, McGraw Hill, 1959.

Prugh, D. G., et al.: Study of emotional reactions of children and their families to hospitalization. *Am. Jour. Orthopsychiatry*, XXIII:70, 1953.

Spence, J. C.: The Care of Children in Hospitals, *The Charles West Lecture*, Royal College of Physicians, 1946.

Spitz, R.: Hospitalism, *Psychoanalytic Study of Child*, I:53, 1945.

Weinstein, E. A., and Kahn, R. L.: *Denial of Illness*. Springfield, Thomas, 1955.

Chapter VIII

The Crises of Adolescence

THE PERIOD of adolescence, covering approximately and variably the years of life from thirteen to twenty, is a major transitional period. During these years the individual is biologically transformed from a child into an adult.

This transformation is associated with greatly increased stimuli originating both internally and externally. New feelings are aroused and new social problems are presented. The body image changes, and intensified sexual impulses disturb the emotional homeostasis. This internal instability is often expressed in lability of mood, and transitory periods of depression are not uncommon during adolescence.

At the same time, the attitudes and expectations of other people toward the adolescent create external pressure. Family attitudes both emphasize and deny the changes in him, vacillating between expectation of mature and responsible behavior and, on the other hand, continuation in the dependent and conforming relationship with the parents. As a result, there is much conflict and confusion in child-parent relationships during this period.

Outside the family, within the child's peer group, competitive pressures increase. The insecurity of the individual favors critical comparisons and strivings for dominance within the group. Standards of behavior, of dress and of ideas are established with rigid insistence on uniformity. There is a need to reinforce strength through group identification, which often results in a sacrifice of individual values for those determined by the pseudo-sophisticated defenses of the dominant clique. It often happens that the child's school milieu shifts, at this time, from a relatively familiar and small grade school set-up to a large and impersonal high school wherein friends may be separated and teachers are less closely related to pupils. Standards of scholastic achievement are raised, and the student is faced with questions of preparation for college or for work.

These intensified internal and external stimuli, following the relative equilibrium of earlier childhood, stir up conflicts similar to those which were experienced in the years of transition from infancy. Then it was necessary that the child modify his intense and possessive attachment to his parents, accept his place as a family member and turn his attention to the larger social group. In adolescence, the old infantile conflicts of dependence-independence and of close erotic attachment are revived. The degree of success which an individual has had in making the earlier transition will influence his success in adaptation to problems of adolescence. If he has been able to achieve a sense of identity apart from his parents while retaining a mutually honest and affectionate relationship with them he is favorably disposed to deal with his new situations. The character structure which he has built determines his adaptive and defensive responses.

A high level of stress in adolescence tests the child's defensive capacities. If the internal and external pressures strain his adaptive resources, evidences of disequilibrium may emerge. Symptoms of anxiety and/or compensatory efforts often become evident at this time or there may be tendencies to regression and withdrawal. The anxiety is sometimes denied by an attitude of bravado and rebelliousness or, in contrast, it can propel the individual into excessive and rigid conformity with renunciation of the "frivolous" and emphasis on the "serious" side of life. Gang-approved standards may be allowed to dominate behavior at the expense of originality and flexibility. If the individual's capacities for interpersonal interaction are relatively good, his disturbance will be limited. When the ego defenses are relatively weak, the symptoms of imbalance may create various disorders.

Disequilibrium may be thought of around a concept of psychic energies. One can speak of internal psychic activity as having energies and forces which were originally sexual or aggressive but diverted by the ego into various ego activities. Such energies are called neutral. Under conditions of stress there is regression and they cease to be neutral and become once more primitive, sexual or aggressive energy. This concept of deneutralization is used as a way of explaining the extremely primitive character of psychic processes in severe regressed states, such as acute schizophrenia.* We have observed that the withdrawn adolescent sometimes develops permanent reactions of social maladaptation and in extreme cases shows, at this age, the first symptoms of schizophrenic psychosis. We have also observed the fact that excessive rebellion in this period of life can create a permanent pattern of delinquency and social alienation.

The tasks of the adolescent are: first, to resolve his problems related to independence versus dependence; second, to define satisfactorily his identity as a young man or young woman rather than as a boy or girl child; third, to integrate his intensified sexual feelings in a manner acceptable to himself and others. These tasks cannot be carried out in a vacuum and they involve much interaction with family and other authoritative figures and with the peer group.

The struggle for independent identity begins, of course, in infancy. It is more obvious at certain early stages of development as, for example, during the so-called "negative" period, at the age of approximately three, when the child's "No!" responses are exaggerated and again when he breaks away from the close "Oedipal" attachment to the parents. But throughout childhood, despite somewhat self-assertive behavior, the boy and girl under ordinary circumstances remain closely related to the family, sharing their attitudes and drawing strength — or weakness — from identification with them. With adolescent development the individual feels an increased need to function independently and, in trying to achieve this, he begins to look at his parents with a detached and often exaggerated objectivity. His parent's faults — real or projected — provide him with a rationalization for rejecting them. By taking issue with them, he feels himself to be a separate individual. The issues may involve any aspect of the family's way of life but they are especially concerned with the degree of freedom of action allowed the adolescent.

This struggle for autonomy, which is a normal aspect of the

*Hartmann, H.: Contributions to the metapsychology of schizophrenia. *Psychoanalytic Study of the Child,* VIII:177, 1953.

growing up process, creates a diversity of behavior patterns determined by cultural traditions, the feelings and attitudes of the parents and child, and the influence of the peer group. In our heterogeneous Western culture there are no fixed standards for adolescent behavior and for this reason, parents tend to vacillate concerning restrictions and demands. They are torn between the wish to hold the child in close conformity and the wish to see him successfully adjusted within his own age group. These ambivalent parental attitudes are expressed in various ways, determined to a large extent by the parent's own adolescent experiences.

A father who had been rejected by and withdrawn from his schoolmates showed much hostility about his fifteen year old daughter's out-going activities. His attitude toward her friends was one of (unacknowledged) jealousy; he was irritable and critical of them and of her. He seemed especially suspicious of her boy friends and seemed incapable of seeing the girl's point of view. The girl's mother, who had better empathy with her, felt that it was necessary to align herself surreptitiously with her daughter to allow a reasonable degree of socialization. This created a secretive home atmosphere and generated a good deal of guilt in the mother.

In contrast, it is often observed that parents whose own adolescence was over-protected or deprived try to realize vicariously through their children their own rebellious strivings.* A son is remonstrated with but subtly admired for his early sexual experimentations and his identification with an aggressive gang. The daughter reacts to the parent's covert encouragement of her "super sophisticated" teenage ways of behaving, even of her involvement in sexual activities.

Parents whose early activities were unrestrained and unprotected often show a tendency to protect their children from the involvements in drinking, promiscuity and the like which they now look back on as destructive in their own lives. In attempting protective measures such parents may, however, insist upon un-

---

*Johnson, A. M.: Sanctions for superego lacunae of adolescents. Eissler, K. (Editor); *Searchlights on Delinquency.* New York, International Universities Press, 1949. Also with Szurek, S. A.: In *Psychoanalytic Quart.,* 21:323, 1952.

realistically rigid standards which confuse and anger their children.

The adolescent himself also reacts in a great variety of ways in the process of struggling for independence. His need to be free of authority-figures expresses itself in exaggerated narcissism and somewhat overt defiance of expectations. He is sloppy and disorganized, lacking in consideration or respect for adults, and inclined to quibble about his "rights." Under this defensive behavior, however, is a need for help from parents in establishing standards. If the parents are too restrictive and protective they are regarded as tyrants and labeled as "old fashioned"; if they are too permissive, the child may feel uneasily that they are not sufficiently concerned about him. It has been repeatedly observed that highly disturbed sociopathic young people who have been hospitalized respond best to a combination of firm and consistent definition of limits plus sincere attempts at understanding on the part of the therapists who work with them.

The problem of dependency in our culture is complicated by the fact that the son and daughter often remain financially obligated to the parents well into early adult life. If the parents can respect the child's autonomy and can support him financially without making excessive emotional demands on him, there need not be unfavorable consequences. The situation often becomes quite involved, however, as illustrated by the following history.

A medical student in his junior year came for counseling because of marital difficulties. He had been married at twenty-one, at the end of his freshman year, to a girl of the same age who had just been graduated from college. For one year she worked and supported her husband but then she became pregnant and it was necessary that they turn to their families for financial help. This brought out problems of disagreement between the wife and her mother-in-law. The young man's mother began more and more to show possessive and controlling attitudes, and the young couple could not deal easily with this because of their feeling of financial dependency. The young wife had welcomed, though she had not planned for, the pregnancy, but she felt guilty about her pleasure in the baby and felt that she should be supporting her husband. Her family implied that she should have married a man able to support her, and this created a certain degree of dissatisfaction in her concerning her marriage. The young man, to supplement help from the family, had to get a part time job and he felt resentful and overworked. While working at this job he met a nurse who developed a good deal of "motherly" interest in him and they became involved in a sexual affair.

His wife threatened a divorce; the husband panicked at this threat, and said he felt unable to give up either his wife, his mother, or the nurse.

This problem illustrates the persistence of childhood dependency and the fortification of this dependency both by the parents' financial support and by the stress and strain of increasing demands for adult responsibility.

The dependence-independence question often comes up in relation to a father's wish that his son, or son-in-law, carry on the father's business or profession. This works out well if an adult-to-adult relationship exists and if the standards and motivations of father and son are in accord. The passive young man who submits to domination for the sake of economic security lacks self respect. He may displace his hostility on to his wife, or it may come out indirectly in inefficiency at work, illness, depressed attitudes, alcoholism, or any number of neurotic reactions.

Similarly, the girl who remains in too close and subordinate attachment to her mother may never break away from the parental home. If she does marry, she may continue to defer to her mother's judgment, to the justified resentment of her husband.

Success in these relationships is determined by a satisfactory resolution of the Oedipal phase of development. We have discussed the early need of the child for both parents which, with greater self and sexual awareness, becomes modified by a tendency to possessive attachment to the opposite-sex parent, and vacillation between competition and identification with the same-sex parent. A good resolution of the possessive-competitive strivings is based on identification of son with the father and daughter with the mother. Adolescence tests the quality of this identification. If it is established on genuine mutual regard, rather than on fear and insecurity, it forms the basis for a good relationship between adolescent and parent and, even more important, for a smooth transition into a relatively independent and responsible adult role.

Especially handicapping to adult development is a continuation, overtly or in fantasy, of the original Oedipal attachment. The son's persistent emotional involvement with his mother, and the daughter's with her father, make a mature love relationship difficult and interfere with the achievement of an independent adult role, as we have previously observed.

The intensification of the problems of individual and sexual identification during adolescence contributes largely to the turmoil of this age period. As an expression of this turmoil, there is a good deal of concentration of difficulty in the area of sexual behavior. Acting out of sexual impulse results from the resurgence of these feelings at this time, but also results from the need of the boy to prove his masculinity, and the need of the girl to be desired. In both cases there is the wish to appear sophisticated, to "know what it's all about" and consequently feel one's self a part of the "in" group.

Such acting out creates practical problems, especially for the girl. A tolerant sexual attitude may seem to contribute to her popularity; however, if she carries it too far her contemporaries may deprecate her as "too easy," or as "a tramp." Also, she is faced, of course, with the risk of pregnancy. Her prospects for making a good marriage are diminished if she too easily assents to intimate relationships during dating. Unreasonable as it is, there does exist the double standard which influences the young man in his selection of a wife.

These practical considerations affecting the adolescent girl constitute only one part of her quandary. She must live with herself, and the nature of her self-image is influenced by her sexual behavior. This image, in turn, influences her futher behavior. In most cases, the girl is not driven so much by sexual needs per se, as by her narcissistic need to be wanted, loved, caressed, and given to. The female is ordinarily more discriminating in her sexual reactions than is the male, less accepting of sexual pleasure merely for its own sake. Her involvement in sexual affairs, therefore, causes her a good deal of confusion. The degree of overt guilt varies, depending upon her family and religious standards. If the parents seem covertly to encourage her acting out, her attitude may seem to be free of guilt but in such cases, the girl may resent the parents' (unacknowledged) attitudes and may tend to project blame on them for not protecting her. If, on the other hand, the parents are strict and repressive, the girl's behavior may be the expression of defiance by which she takes satisfaction in humiliating them. If she feels deeply rejected by her family she may be seeking blindly to secure love and attention, using the devices at her disposal. This is one of the commonest motivations for sexual acting out in girls. They express it to a counselor by saying that they did not really enjoy the experience but they liked the closeness and the attention which it gave them.

The boy involved in sexual affairs feels more social sanction of his behavior and is not as vulnerable as the girl to either practical or psychic penalties. The cultural emphasis on masculine vigor and aggression contributes to pride in sexual achievement. He faces, of course, the possibility of being "caught" in an early marriage and the more sensitive young man may become early too involved emotionally with his steady girl friend to be able to break away even while he resents her possessiveness.

The parents of the adolescent are involved, more or less intensely, in the sexual crises of this period, but their ability to guide and influence their children is no longer as effective as it was in earlier years. The effects of the early parent-child relationship will, however, determine, in large part, the nature of the rebellious or cooperative interaction that goes on at this time.

Normally, much of the sexual stress of the pre-adolescent or early adolescent years is dissipated by activities with others of the same age and sex or in mixed groups. Interest in sports and other extra-curricular recreational projects is helpful. Some communities offer a good many organized activities of this kind.

The adolescent's capacity for acceptance of sexual self-control depends on early conditioning. One with an emotionally deprived childhood may use sexual lovemaking as a compensatory experience. The patterns of behavior often reflect attitudes to which the child has been exposed in his family. Frank exhibition of sexual interest between the parents is overly stimulating during the child's latency period. Seductive attitudes or behavior toward the child by family members, or by any older individuals, absorb energies that should, during the pre-adolescent years, be directed elsewhere. Such overly stimulated children find the impact of their intensified adolescent sexuality overwhelming. In reality and/or in fantasy they are obsessed by it, often to the neglect of other interests.

In contrast to the young people who act out their sexual impulses, there are many who excessively repress and deny them, or express them only in secretive fantasy and masturbation. This unrealistically repressed attitude may indicate an inadequate resolution of the Oedipal relationship with the parents. The incest taboo, which made sexual feeling for a parent unacceptable, makes the feeling itself unacceptable regardless of its object. Fear of parental wrath and disapprobation may be exaggerated far beyond the degree to which it actually exists. This inhibition and denial of a developmental process creates tension and unhappiness in the adolescent. If he attempts to relieve this tension by auto-erotic activities he is often beset by a strong sense of guilt and shame which interferes with healthy, out-going social integration.

We have described the first developmental periods of life as "oral" (dependent, incorporating) and "anal" (aggressive, resistant) followed by the "Oedipal" period of greater awareness of sexual identity. During the succeeding latency period of childhood the intensity of the oral, anal, and sexually possessive strivings tends to diminish and to be sublimated in group activities. The adolescent, then, must integrate the residues of these early strivings into a more mature pattern of close interpersonal relationships. The longing for dependence and exclusiveness carried over from the parent-child relationships favors such customs as "going steady." Also, dependence on the group has about it an almost oral quality. The aggression and defiance of the anal phase are evident, at this time, most clearly in the intensified struggle against authority. It shows itself also in emphasis on possessiveness and domination in sexual relationships which, if persistent, may interfere with emergence of the tender, considerate, and sharing feelings which must be the bases for good marriage. As we go on to study the processes involved in evolution from adolescence to maturity, we shall see again the individual struggling with these early motivations as he faces the problem of attaining a responsible vocational and family role.

SUMMARY

Adolescence is the period of development during which the individual tests his capacities for independent functioning. He must at this time break the close bonds with his parents, establish goals for adult life, and form satisfying social and sexual relationships. The self concepts and the behavior patterns which he has already formed influence the degree of success he will achieve in making these adaptations. The confusions and ambivalences which are characteristic of the adolescent phase are ordinarily transitory but they may become the basis for serious and persistent psychopathology.

SUGGESTED READINGS

Blos, P.: *On Adolescence.* New York, Free Press of Glencoe, 1962.

Eissler, K. R.: Problems of technique in treatment of adolescents. *Psychoanalytic Study of the Child,* XIII:223, 1958.

Freud, A.: Adolescence. *Psychoanalytic Study of the Child,* XIX:255, 1958.

Geleerd, E. R.: Ego vicissitudes in adolescence. *J. Amer. Psychoanalytic Ass'n,* IX, 1961.

Gitelson, M.: The psychotherapeutic problem of adolescence. *Amer. J. Orthopsychiatry,* XVIII, 1948.

Jacobson, Edith: Adolescent moods. *Psychoanalytic Study of the Child,* XVI:164, 1962.

Josselyn, I. M.: *The Adolescent and His World.* New York, Family Service Ass'n of America, 1952.

Lampl-De Groot, J.: On adolescence. *Psychoanalytic study of the Child,* XV:95, 1960.

Root, N.: A neurosis in adolescence. *Psychoanalytic Study of the Child,* XII:320, 1957.

Spiegel, L. A.: Psychology of adolescents. *Psychoanalytic Study of the Child,* XIII:296, 1958, VI, 1951.

Chapter IX

The Genesis of Neurotic Anxiety

THE DEVELOPMENTAL disturbances which we have been describing — feeding inhibitions, overly aggressive or overly withdrawn behavior, learning blocks, compulsive and paranoid attitudes, sexual maladjustment — could all be described as neurotic reactions. They are handicapping and limiting disorders of function brought about not primarily by organ damage, but rather by the child's unsatisfactory social experience.

Neurosis is not a sharply defined syndrome. It is a state of maladjustment which may take many forms and express itself in many degrees of severity. Certainly we cannot separate children or adults into well defined categories of neurotic and non-neurotic. We might say that any individual is relatively free of neurosis insofar as he accepts himself with equanimity and is able to make full use of his potentialities in ways that are acceptable to himself and to society. A child is neurotic if he is so handicapped by confusions and conflicts in his interpersonal relationships that he cannot achieve a sense of internal stability or an ability to express himself constructively.

The symptoms which such a child develops can make us aware of his emotional state and may give us clues as to its meaning.

The most frank and direct expression of emotional disequilibrium is seen in symptoms of excessive anxiety.

Obviously anxiety need not be neurotic. Everyone experiences it frequently in relation to threatening and confusing life situations. It is neurotic only insofar as it is realistically excessive or occurs in the absence of a recognizable external danger. Under these circumstances the reaction is not a transparent cause-and-effect phenomenon but rather an indication of the patient's conflictual and insecure attitudes.

116

Anxiety has been called* a signal of threat either external or internal. It is a state of painful disequilibrium which demands relief. In case of external danger the appropriate response is action to remove the threat. When the threat is an internal one, only vaguely if at all consciously perceived, the person will strive for a new equilibrium through some kind of symptom formation. The kind of symptom will be determined by the character structure of the individual.

In the child, anxiety tends to attach itself to specific situations, resulting in the formation of phobias. It often can be seen to be related to some particular frightening experience. In other cases it reflects the anxiety of adults close to the child. For example, a child may be especially anxious about dogs because he has been jumped on and hurt by a dog or, in the absence of any such frightening experience, he may have developed a reaction in response to his mother's cautioning and frightened attitude about animals. Sometimes the object of the fright may be understood only if one can trace its association.

> A four-year-old boy suddenly expressed a great fear of frogs or of anything that reminded him of them. An interview with the boy's father brought out the fact that he had been reading to the boy a story about a big bull frog in the course of which the father spoke in a deep voice and "croaked" like a frog. Also, the father had observed that the child recently seemed anxious when father and son took shower baths together. The child had been clinging more to his mother and seemed uneasy in his father's presence. Here the Oedipal competition with the father and its resulting anxieties had apparently been transferred to the frog by a process of association.

We do not often see in children the acute anxiety panics which are common as expressions of emotional disequilibrium in adults. Most often the anxiety focuses either in phobic situations such as we have described or is expressed somatically.

The somatic expressions of anxiety are any of the vegetative reactions characteristic of a state of fear: rapid heart, gastro-intestinal disturbances, trembling, dizziness, restlessness, inter-

*Freud, S.: *The Problem of Anxiety*. New York, W. W. Norton Co., 1936.

ferences with appetite and sleep. Such symptoms may simulate organic disease. The observant physician, however, will notice an accompanying state of fearfulness in the child out of proportion to the objective symptoms.

Attacks of vomiting on an emotional basis are common in children and are often mis-diagnosed. It is important that the doctor get a clear impression of the child's interactions with his family if symptoms such as this are to be adequately treated.

Excessive anxiety may become characteristic of a child's way of reacting and may determine, to a large extent, his life as an adult. Being overly cautious and uncertain he avoids adventure and change, chooses the safe and well established routine. His free-floating anxiety attaches itself to one situation or another and he becomes a "worrier." Hypochondriacal tendencies (preoccupation with fears of illness) may begin in childhood. The child thinks of himself as weak and vulnerable, concentrates on his bodily sensations and avoids many of the normal, outgoing activities of his age group. Attitudes of this kind, if not overcome, persist into adult life and interfere seriously with the development of a free and flexible personality pattern.

The anxiety syndrome is a mass reaction of the organism to a situation of danger. As has been said, this "danger" may be external or may be an internal and not consciously recognized turmoil. The reaction pattern is universal in all human beings and in many animals as well. Cannon[1] has described it as the "fight or flight" pattern. The organism mobilizes its resources for aggression or for running away. The rapid heart, the dilated pupils, temporarily suspended gastrointestinal absorption, rise in blood pressure and blood sugar, all suggest such mobilization. However, in most human cases neither fight nor flight is possible and there usually is no clearly defined adversary with whom one can struggle or from whom one can escape. In neurotic anxiety the danger is one's own sense of instability or lack of control.

The child therefore, in his symptoms of excessive anxiety, indicates his feeling of uncertainty and insecurity in his life situation. The imaginative, sensitive child has a greater prone-

---

[1]Cannon, W. B.: *The Wisdom of the Body.* New York, W. W. Norton, 1932.

ness to anxiety because he senses, more acutely than does the stolid child, the inconsistencies and unreliabilities of his environment. Particularly, he responds to unsure ambivalent feelings in his parents. If he has developed a strong moral sense he is vaguely aware of the conflicts that exist between his impulses and his conscience, and this creates in him a sense of disequilibrium which expresses itself in anxiety.

The doctor who observes neurotic anxiety in a young patient should look first into the overt nature of the child-parent relationship. If the parents are overly protective and anxious people, it may be helpful to make them aware of the disturbing effect of their attitudes on the child.

In some cases the child's anxiety may be traced to a specific frightening event which he has been unable to comprehend and accept. His free-floating anxiety may represent his attempt to defend himself against further hurt. Children tend to repress painful experiences and they may deny that anything has disturbed them. Parents often report that they are surprised by the apparent lack of reaction of a child to death or other crises in the family. The disturbance shows itself, however, in indirect ways.

Neurotic anxiety in some children is related not so much to specific frightening experiences as to a sense of internal turmoil. The disturbance indicates a state of conflict among opposing impulses. Thus the child with strong superego development may show anxiety under circumstances which tempt him to express aggression; one with well developed loyalties to his parents is upset by his angry and rebellious feelings toward them.

The situation is analogous to that of laboratory animals with an experimentally induced neurosis. Pavlov's[1] work with dogs and Masserman's work with cats demonstrate the mechanisms involved. Pavlov's animals, for example, were conditioned to respond positively to a slow metronome beat, this beat being associated with the giving of food. The same animals were conditioned to a negative response to a fast metronome which was accompanied by a painful shock. It was then demonstrated that

---

[1]Pavlov, I.: *Lectures on Conditioned Reflexes.* New York, International Publishers, 1928.

as the metronome beat approached a middle speed the dogs showed symptoms of apparent anxiety. They were unable to discriminate between their opposing impulses and became, under these circumstances, disorganized and disturbed.

When anxiety is responded to by specific somatic symptoms having a symbolic meaning, the process is called "conversion" and the condition is called "conversion hysteria." The symptoms differ from those we have just described in being less frankly expressive of anxiety and in the fact that they tend to involve the sensory-motor rather than the vegtative system. They include anesthesias, paralyses, convulsive movements, contractures, disturbances of the special senses, such as transitory blindness or deafness, and they may include such vegetative symptoms as vomiting or coughing. Conversion symptoms are not common in children and are, in fact, no longer frequently seen in adult psychiatric practice. This is the type of neurosis that was commonly described a hundred years ago and seems now to be largely replaced by the less bizarre vegetative disturbances. It is, however, occasionally seen in older children, and a correct diagnosis is important because of its confusing similarity to organic illness.

The child with conversion hysteria symptoms differs from the anxiously disturbed child we have been describing in that there is less overt emotionality. The symptom of blindness or paralysis or vomiting is usually not associated with a generalized state of anxious turmoil; it may occur in an apparently calm child.

The symbolic nature of conversion symptoms is indicated by the fact that the organ involved does not react according to anatomic and physiologic expectations. An hysterical anesthesia of an arm, for example, does not follow the nerve distribution but rather is patterned after the person's concept of his arm or his hand, being sharply demarcated at the wrist or shoulder.

Convulsive seizures on a hysterical basis differ from epilepsy in their more bizarre movements and in the fact that the patient does not become incontinent nor bite the tongue nor show neurologic signs. He seldom hurts himself. The behavior during a seizure is often suggestive of sexual or aggressive movements. In children it may appear to be an exaggerated temper tantrum.

We have seen that neurotic anxiety symptoms emerge in the

child as a frank expression of disequilibrium. The symptoms are those that anyone experiences in a threatening situation and they therefore need have no specific individual meaning. If they become attached to an object and a phobia develops, the choice of phobia does have a relationship to the child's experiences. It symbolizes the source of his fear. It is as though he focuses all the anxiety on the object or situation and then avoids it, thus limiting and circumscribing the area of his anxiety.

A conversion symptom has a similar neurotic purpose. It constitutes an attempt to resolve a conflict. This conflict, as in all neurotic states, exists between repressed and repressing elements in the personality. Feelings, impulses to act, curiosities arising in the child, are repressed because of intimidation, disapproval by others or self-disapproval.

Repression is a normal and universal process, as we have seen, and as long as it functions smoothly all goes well. Circumstances may occur, however, in the life of a child or an adult which may disrupt the equilibrium in either of two ways. The repressed element may be excessively stimulated or the repressing forces may be weakened. For example, a ten-year-old child's repressed longings for infantile dependency may be fortified by a long period of illness or, in another instance, his capacity to repress these longings may be weakened by experiences which destroy his self-confidence and which make him doubt his capacity for more adult behavior. A similar conflict might arise in relation to repressed aggressive impulses or to repressed sexual curiosity. The repressed tendencies, under these circumstances, tend to emerge, and at times they do so frankly in regressive behavior of some kind. The child's self-disapproval may defend against frank regression and may lead to a kind of compromise symptomatology as it does in conversion states. This process may arise out of conflict on any level of development. The symptom allows the repressed element to express itself, but in a displaced and distorted way. Or, in contrast, the symptom represents symbolically the strengthening of repression against the impulse. Paralysis and anesthesia represent intensified repression; convulsions and contractures may be a distorted expression of the repressed impulse.

A.B., a girl of fourteen, was brought in from Neurology with symptoms of numbness and weakness of both legs which had been persistent for the past six weeks. The history was that about two months before she had been seduced by a boy two years older than herself. Following this experience the girl seemed very depressed for a few days, then developed the present symptoms.

She was an only girl in a family with two brothers, one older and one younger than herself. She is reported to have always been extremely close to her father, who spent much time with this child. The mother had turned the children over to the father and spent little time with them, but rather spent a great deal of time with her own mother toward whom she was very dependent.

A. was an attractive girl, but childish for her age. She had shown little interest in boys, and had tended to devote herself to her studies. She stated that she wanted to be a lawyer like her father. Her older brother had early experimented in sexual behavior and in drinking, and was in every way a contrast to this girl.

The precipitating situation was that of an experience one evening when she was home alone and the neighbor boy came over to help her with her studies. He succeeded in having partial intercourse with her. Following this incident he did not return for several days and seemed to be avoiding her. During this period she was very depressed. He then came back and again tried to seduce her, and it was following this second experience that she developed the symptoms of numbness and weakness in her legs.

It seemed apparent that this girl had developed a strong defense against sexuality, which was related to her close attachment to her father. She had avoided mature sexual behavior and had tried to remain on a childish level as a good little girl of whom father would approve. Her sexual feelings were aroused at the time of the first experience but she developed a great deal of conflict about this. The depression when she felt ignored by the boy indicated her strong longings in the direction of sexual experience, but her guilt when he did return created a violent defense against the impulse which was unacceptable to her. This defense took a somatic symbolic form in the numbness and weakness of the legs.

A symptom not infrequently seen in pediatric practice is the muscular tic. This could be considered as a form of conversion hysteria in that it is a somatic disturbance indicating emotional stress and strain. It occurs most commonly in children of about five to ten and is usually of relatively short duration, but sometimes it may persist chronically into adult life. The twitching movements most commonly involve muscles of the face, neck and shoulders though other parts of the body may be involved. Spasmodic blinking of the eyes, jerking of the head, grimacing of the mouth are common tics. The hands and arms often participate in a repetitive gesture involving also head and neck movements. In some patients the movements are elaborate and are frequently repeated, constituting a serious handicap; in others they are less diffuse and less noticeable. In every case they tend to follow a repetitive pattern with little variation. It may often be observed that they are intensified when the child is in a stressful situation; however, once established, they may occur periodically without obvious precipitating factors.

The diagnosis of tic is ordinarily quite obvious. Occasionally the movements may simulate those of Sydenham's chorea but close observation discloses a more specific patterning of the tic; the chorea being more a diffuse, generalized motor disturbance.

The tic appears to represent a kind of overflow of repressed aggressive activity. It develops particularly in the child who does not readily act out his feelings. His inhibited state may be the result of frank intimidation. In other cases it reflects the overprotective, cautious attitudes of the parents and is influenced by a social milieu which disapproves of violence. Sometimes the movements seem quite clearly to have a symbolic meaning similar to that of other conversion symptoms. This may represent an avoidance as by blinking the eyes or turning the head away, or it may appear to be a gestural kind of expression of aggression as in jerking movements of the hand and arms.

As is true of many neurotic symptoms, the tic once established intensifies the child's problems of adaptation. It makes him appear "queer" and vulnerable to the taunts of his associates and, in this way, it adds to his anger and isolation.

A fourteen-year-old boy was referred to Psychiatry from the medical service because of apparently involuntary movement of his arms which continued whenever he was awake. His medical history and physical examination were not diagnostic of Sydenham's chorea, and no organic pathology was discovered. On initial examination the boy seemed very resistive and uncommunicative, but later was able to talk more freely about his feelings. His history indicated that since the death of the boy's father when the child was five he had been reared by his mother and grandmother who were very competitive with each other for his affections, and imposed a good deal of inconsistent discipline on him. As he grew older and tried to rebel against the over-protection of the two mothers, he was inhibited by feelings of guilt and loyalty. Unable to express his aggression directly, he expressed it symbolically in aggressive movements. After he had been encouraged to speak more freely and to understand his feelings, and after his mother and grandmother had gained some insight into the meaning of the problem, the symptom disappeared.

Treatment of the child with a tic aims at more spontaneous expression of feelings on the part of the child and less restraint on him by his family. Admonition to voluntary control of the symptoms is not only useless, but it increases the child's tension.

The same principles of treatment apply to the child with other symptoms of conversion hysteria except that some hysterical symptoms are more transient and more amenable to direct suggestion therapy than is the tic. We may think of symptoms as differing in the degree to which they become an integral part of the patient's personality. Anxiety, for example, may be acute and episodic in relation to a traumatic situation, or it may become a character pattern representative of the person's basic attitudes toward himself and the world. A tic, because of its undeviating, repetitive pattern, tends to become incorporated into the patient's image of himself; whereas the hysterical paralysis or contracture or convulsion may be regarded more as a superimposed illness. In any case, whatever the neurotic symptoms are they indicate the need for careful study of the child in his intimate environment with the aim of alleviating internal and external stresses which are causing the disequilibrium.

SUMMARY

The child is predisposed to neurotic anxiety by experiences which make him insecure or by internal conflicts which he cannot understand or with which he cannot deal directly. Such anxiety may express itself psychosomatically or it may be translated into phobias or conversion symptoms, or it may influence the formation of fearful, restrictive personality traits. Successful treatment depends on early diagnosis of the symptoms and recognition of the etiologic factors.

SUGGESTED READINGS

Abse, D. W.: *The Diagnosis of Hysteria.* Bristol, Wright, 1950.

Cobb, S.: *Emotions and Clinical Medicine.* New York, W. W. Norton, 1950.

Freud, S.: *Inhibitions, Symptoms, and Anxiety.* Trans. by Shacky, A., London, Hogarth Press, 1936.

Gerard, M.: The psychogenic tic in ego development, *Psychoanalytic Study of Child,* 2:133, 1947.

Gerard, M.: Genesis of Psychosomatic Symptons in Infancy, The Influence of Infantile Traumata Upon Sympton Choice in *The Psychosomatic Concept in Psychoanalysis,* Felix Deutch, Ed., New York, Int. Univ. Press, 1953.

Hoch, P. and Zubin, J.: *Anxiety,* New York, Grune & Stratton, 1950.

Kepecs, J. G.: Some patterns of somatic displacement, *Psychosomatic Med.,* 15:425, 1953.

Lippman, H. S.: *Treatment of the Child in Emotional Conflict.* 2nd Ed., New York, McGraw Hill, 1962.

Mahler, M. S.: Tic in the psychopathology of children, *Psychoanalytic Study of Child,* 3/4:279, 1949.

Miller, H., and Baruch, D. W.: Psychosomatic studies of children with allergic manifestations, *Psychosomatic Med.,* 10:275, 1948.

Proctor, J. T.: Hysteria in childhood, *Am. J. Ortho.,* 28:394, 1958.

Sperling, M.: The role of the mother in psychosomatic disorders in children, *Psychosomatic Med.,* II:377, 1949.

Chapter X

Adaptation to Maturation

FROM THE moment of birth the human being must make adaptations, physiologic or psychologic, to his environment. He must adapt to cold, to pain, hunger, infection, physical injury, to fright, loneliness, neglect, and the demands of other people upon him.

On a physiologic level of operation the body manages, under ordinary circumstances, to preserve a steady state regardless of changes in physical surroundings. The temperature, blood pressure and blood count vary somewhat in response to unusual stimuli but tend generally to stay within safe limits and to reestablish normalcy promptly.

In acute crisis, the organism responds by mobilizing the body's defenses against the pathogenic factor. This leads to such defensive reactions as fever, white blood cell count increase, proliferation of connective tissue. When the crisis is not extreme, as in non-virulent infections, these acute defensive reactions serve well to overcome the assault, and body equilibrium is reestablished. A long continued or overwhelming disease may, however, exhaust the defensive resources and allow a breakdown of vital functions. Also, the processes of defense may, by their own excessive degree, create additional danger for the organism. A too-high fever or too-great overgrowth of tissue may do harm to the body and create new adaptive problems.

The adaptive responses of the person as a social unit follow principles similar to these. Faced with a crisis in social interaction the person tends to respond with alarm, to mobilize psychological defenses (acute neurotic reactions) and, finally, if the difficulties overtax his resources, to capitulate via regression to a state of chronic neurotic or psychotic illness.

Here, too, the defensive symptoms may in themselves constitute the overt illnesses: may handicap rather than heal. We see this in the animal who "freezes" in response to danger. His immobility may have a protective purpose by making him less visible and less stimulating to his enemy, but it paralyzes his capacity to fight or to flee. Similarly, in human beings, the mass reaction to threat which we have described as anxiety paralyzes the capacity for clear thinking and resourceful activity. It adds to the original (often unconscious) trauma its own extremely distressing subjective symptoms. In further defensive effort the anxious person, unable to deal directly with his adaptation problem, may use the inefficient and unrealistic reactions that we recognize as psychiatric illness.

The person as a social unit must make two kinds of adaptations. He must adjust himself first to the biological processes of maturation, and second to the expectations of his social milieu. In other words, he must accept the need to grow up and to live cooperatively with other people.

It might seem that maturation poses no problem: that the child develops as a rose unfolds. For the most part this, of course, is true. The child tends to reach out progressively for new skills, new learning, greater freedom and responsibility. But we have seen as we have been reviewing the problems of development that there is much ambivalence in this process. The child wants to grow but he also wants to cling to old satisfactions. He resists weaning, toilet training, relinquishment of dependence. He resists the necessity to substitute social codes for the purely selfish motivations of behavior. He may even resist learning and assume a retarded attitude.

The problems of biologic maturation are closely related to the necessities for social adaptation. This we have seen clearly in our discussion of feeding and toilet training. Feeding behavior and toilet training as developmental processes become confused with issues of dominance or subordination, with the child's willfulness in conflict with authority.

The adult neurotic person has been described as one tied to the past, seeking in his life situation for the gratification he prized as a child. He craves dependency and is insatiable in his demands for reassurance, though he may deny and disguise these needs in manifold ways. He is still struggling with the problem of authority, and expresses his chronic rebellion in behavior often detrimental to his own goals. He may still be obsessed by the sexual curiosities and conflicts of his childhood, and thus handicapped in establishing a mature, close love relationship. He has remained fixed in these early preoccupations because he has not developed efficient and realistic patterns of adaptation.

The attainment of adult status, therefore, implies a relatively satisfactory mastery of the adaptive problems of infancy, childhood and adolescence. Each of these periods we have seen as overlapping with and dependent on the previous period. The infant's task has been to define himself as a separate and significant individual, self-expressive yet cognizant of the limitations imposed by his environment. During early childhood he has struggled with strongly ambivalent erotized feelings about his parents and has somewhat successfully accepted his place in the family. Insofar as this has been accomplished, he has then been free to turn his attention to socialization within his peer group. The attitudes toward himself and others which he learned within the close milieu of his family now provide the foundations for group integration. During the crises of adolescence, all adaptive problems have been intensified. Self-awareness is increased as the young person feels the need to emancipate himself from his family and to think and feel independently. The intense emotions of the Oedipal period have been reawakened, and he has again become involved in striving toward intense, intimate love relationships.

Assuming that the individual has accomplished successfully these biologic and social adaptations, he then becomes, we say, a mature person and as such less vulnerable to the conflicts and confusions expressed in neurotic and psychotic reactions. Maturity does not guarantee against psychopathologic reaction to severe social or physiologic trauma in adult life but it makes such reaction less likely.

The mature person is essentially one who is relatively free from the need to use his experiences for self-reassurance. He can therefore see himself with some objectivity in his social milieu and can judge other people with similar objectivity. His activities are motivated not entirely by competitive strivings or strivings for self-aggrandizement but, to a significant degree, by enjoyment in an accomplishment for its own sake. The "taking" (oral) experiences of his childhood have enriched him with knowledge and skill, have stimulated his curiosity, given him confidence. He now, as an adult, has resources of personality that allow him to direct his energies to socially constructive goals without immediate narcissistic rewards. He can have joy in giving as well as in taking. His friendships and love relationships are sharing and deeply emphatic, rather than primarily possessive and dependency-gratifying experiences.

Maturity or the lack of it is clearly revealed by the individual's capacity for good close personal relationships. A person may relate well superficially, have many casual friends and seem to function well socially, yet may exhibit the most immature behavior within his family. This is unfortunate because, as we have observed, unfavorable parental attitudes influence the development of the child. Only a mature parent can provide for his children an environment dictated by the child's welfare rather than by the parent's own anxiety or pride or need for domination. Anyone working therapeutically with disturbed children must work with their parents. If the parents lack the capacity to see the child's point of view, if they are absorbed still in their own need for recognition and self-assurance, progress is difficult. We know how sensitively the child reacts to parental example and how unimportant all other teaching is compared to this. The mature husband and wife in their manifestations of love for each other create in their children an awareness of the quality of a good heterosexual relationship. This is a most valuable heritage.

Maturity is an ideal of self-acceptance and social conscientiousness. Its satisfactory achievement depends on the experiences that have gone before and it, in turn, determines the adaptive processes of the post-mature life. The continuity and the overlapping of phases of development, which we have so repeatedly stressed in our study of early developmental periods, continue to the end of life.

Sociopathic tendencies usually manifest themselves at an early age, though not necessarily to a degree to be easily recognizable as such. A depressive or suspicious attitude, a tendency to withdraw, violent hostilities, or excessive dependency may be masked or sublimated to a passable extent during an active and physically healthy youth and maturity. These tendencies may become apparent only as responses to the restrictions of involution and advancing age.

As one becomes older it becomes more difficult to avoid a frank evaluation of himself in his situation. The fantasies of adolescence and the active strivings of adult years can no longer distract and no longer reassure one of gains to be made in the future. The aging person must see himself for what he is and must accept the way of life which he has established. He must know then that his dreams have been realized or renunciated, and often he must see how far he has come from realization of them, or if this has been attained, how empty and transitory the rewards have been.

The period of involution, like all life periods, cannot be arbitrarily determined. It is associated with changes in hormone activity but the effect of such changes is variable and uncertain. More important are the psychologic resources which are available to deal with the changing life situation. Some people use age as an excuse for narrowing their activities long before this is physiologically indicated. Others, in contrast, fight desperately to avoid any restriction of their activities. Others, more realistically, accept the limitations but continue an alert and creative life well into advanced years.

External circumstances may handicap the post-mature person. Ill health, particularly the degenerative illnesses, may restrict his adaptive capacities. However, these illnesses are adaptive processes and are influenced not only by the constitutional endowment and physical environmental factors but also by stresses involved in interpersonal interactions. Such disabling diseases as arthritis, diabetes and hypertension are affected by the patient's emotional state which can be either a contributing cause of the illness or a determinant of the individual's adaptation to it. Every person has somatic "weak spots" vulnerable to breakdown under strain. The stress that precipitates the break may be physical or psychic or a combination of the two, and the nature of the adaptation made under these circumstances depends on the patterns of response developed in earlier years.

Relative independence of need for constant reassurance has been used as an index of maturity. Such an independent attitude faces increasing difficulties in the later years of life. Physical strength and attractiveness and, to a variable degree, mental alertness diminish with the years. Capacity for useful social contributions is also restricted. The woman whose children are grown and no longer need her, the man who faces retirement from work and displacement by younger people, have a difficult adaptive problem, and they may then develop overt psychiatric symptoms for the first time.

The central nervous system is affected more or less by the aging process, and defects in mental functions may complicate the adaptive problem. These defects are shown in loss of capacity rather than in distortion of reality. Each person adapts *to* and *with* these handicaps according to his character pattern. He may accept the impairment of memory, the confusion in orientation, in a philosophic way, adjusting his life to them, or the frustrations of his handicapped state may be reacted to by neurotic or psychotic defenses. It has often been observed that the aged or otherwise brain-damaged person shows an exaggeration of personality traits which have been characteristic of him throughout life. The suspicious person becomes paranoid; the depressive person, depressed. The withdrawn individual may show schizophrenic symptoms. The man or woman who has attained a relatively mature personality may have serious brain damage, hence marked defect symptoms, but otherwise show no reality distortions.

We have tried to stress throughout this book the continuity of the developmental process and the desirability of smooth progress from one phase to the next. We have seen fixations and regressions as contributing to retardations in growth, and we have observed that the persistence of infantile conflicts into adult life predisposes to pathology. Psychopathological symptoms appear as defenses, as inefficient and unrealistic adaptive responses to environmental demands for which the individual is poorly prepared. This point of view leads one logically to emphasize the importance of the early years of life in establishing the foundations for a well-integrated personality.

Relative freedom from infantile conflicts allows the adult to use his resources more fully and flexibly. It makes him less vulnerable to internal turmoil and social maladjustment. This alone, of course, does not guarantee a full and significant life. Other qualities which we can only descriptively call intelligence, imagination, courage, perceptiveness, creativity, determine the quality of the life pattern. The therapist cannot alter the individual's endowment, but in a supportive and interacting way he can encourage adaptive patterns that allow the fullest degree of self-realization.

Prophylactic psychiatry has in recent years been increasingly concerned with a wider range of family and community problems. This is indicated by the emphasis on establishment of small outlying clinics for child and adult psychiatric care and the integration of the work of such clinics with the medical and sociologic resources of the neighborhoods in which they are situated. Such a diffusion of psychiatric interest should make it possible to more easily recognize the larger cultural deterrants to good mental health. The effects of poverty, ignorance and misunderstanding, mass discouragement and hostility, become evident in the overall view.

The maladjusted child or adult must still be studied as an individual with his own unique intrapersonal problems. At the same time, he can be observed as an interacting unit in a social milieu that often fails to provide him with adequate physical and emotional support, intellectual stimulation, or honest and consistent moral codes.

The nature of the individual's interaction at any period is to a large extent dependent on his state of maturation and his psychologic ontogenesis. It should be recognized that these parameters are subject to scientific study, clinical evaluation, objective analysis. Psychiatric theory and technique establish guides for such a study. The aim, as in all medical procedures, is the achievement of healthier, that is, more efficient, realistic and satisfying, patterns of adaptation.

SUGGESTED READINGS

Arieti, S. (Ed.): *American Handbook of Psychiatry.* New York, Basic Books, 1959.

Association for Research in Nervous and Mental Disease: *Life Stress and Bodily Disease,* Vol. 29, 1950.

Bosselman, B. C.: *Neurosis and Psychosis.* 3rd Ed, Springfield, Thomas, 1964.

Bosselman, B. C.: *The Troubled Mind.* New York, Ronald Press, 1953.

Bosselman, B. C.: *Self Destruction.* Springfield, Thomas, 1958.

First National Conference on Aging, Man and His Years. Raleigh, Health Publications Institute, Inc., 1951.

Glover, E.: *Psychoanalysis: A Handbook for Medical Practitioners and Students of Comparative Psychology.* London, Staples, 1939.

Grinker, R. R. and Spiegel, J. P.: *Men Under Stress.* New York, Blakiston, 1945.

Hoch, P. H., and Zubin, J. (Eds.): *Comparative Epidemiology of Mental Disorders.* New York, Grune & Stratton, 1961.

Hollingshead, A. B. and Redlich, F. C.: *Social Class and Mental Illness.* New York, John Wiley & Sons, 1958.

Kallmann, F. J.: The Genetics of Mental Illness, *American Handbook of Psychiatry.* Arieti, S. (Ed.) New York, Basic Books, 1959.

McFarland, R. A.: The psychological aspects of aging, *Bull. N.Y. Acad. Med.* 1956.

Munroe, R. L.: *Schools of Psychoanalytic Thought.* New York, Dryden Press, 1955.

Selye, H.: *The Stress of Life.* New York, McGraw Hill, 1956.

Saul, L. J.: *Emotional Maturity.* Philadelphia, J. B. Lippincott, 1947.

Index